PIZZAEXPRESS

FROM ITALY WITH LOVE

SEVEN DIALS

CONTENTS

THE START OF A DREAM

In 1965, an Englishman had a dream: to introduce great Italian pizza to the UK. That man was Peter Boizot MBE. Inspired by his travels, he wanted to bring the flavours of Italy closer to home, and the first PizzaExpress was born. The restaurant used authentic ingredients to create proper Italian pizza, cooked in a genuine pizza oven – a simple but radical idea in Sixties London.

Driven by passion, ingenuity and the desire to get a decent pizza in London, Peter wanted his legacy to be not only about food but also the whole UK dining scene. Great food at an affordable price in stylish surroundings – his idea seems straightforward now, but at the time it was ground-breaking and blazed the trail for those that followed.

AND SO IT BEGAN...

As a young man, after finishing school, Peter jumped at the opportunity to spend three months in Italy teaching English to the four children of a wealthy family. It was his first trip to the country and he quickly realised it would not be his last. He immersed himself in the Italian way of life, falling in love with the culture, the people and, of course, the food, which was certainly more colourful and exciting than he'd been used to in his hometown of Peterborough. At a young age, Peter had decided he did not want to eat meat, and the abundance of vegetarian dishes he enjoyed in Italy was a culinary eye-opener. It was on this trip that he was introduced to pizza for the first time. When he told his hosts how he loved watching the pizzaiolos in their striped T-shirts in the local pizzeria, skilfully kneading and tossing the dough, they arranged for their chef to cook homemade pizza. The bright, vibrant colours and the incredible flavours of the dough and mozzarella enthralled him and a life-long love affair began.

After completing his national service and a degree at Cambridge, Peter embarked on an exciting journey, travelling and working all over Europe. Wherever he was, he took in the social scene and enjoyed the music and restaurants. Always on the lookout for great pizzerias, he found them all over Europe and the seeds of an idea started to grow.

Peter returned to Britain in 1965. London was swinging to the songs of The Beatles, girls wore mini-skirts, boys wore flares – and Peter was surprised to find this was the only city in Europe where he couldn't buy a decent pizza. Taking the expert knowledge he had acquired on his travels, he was convinced that he could provide quality, affordable Italian fare to Londoners. All he needed were premises, a proper pizza oven and customers.

The oven came first. Peter knew it was impossible to recreate the authentic taste of Italian pizza without a genuine Italian oven. He flew to Rome and went directly to Signor Notaro, the manufacturer of the oven he wanted to buy. It cost £600 and he arranged for it to be delivered to England, along with a man to operate it.

Strapped for cash after this purchase, Peter went on the search for premises and had a stroke of luck. When he met with the person who was to be his mozzarella supplier – Margaret Zampi, widow of film director Mario Zampi – she told him how she was keen to sell her husband's failing pizzeria, but only to someone who shared his vision of making great pizza in London. The deal was done and 29 Wardour Street, in the heart of London's bustling Soho district, became the first PizzaExpress. The only problem was that when Peter tried to install his prized oven, he found it was so big and so heavy (it weighed a tonne) that it couldn't fit through the door. So what did Peter do? He asked some friends to help out and they knocked the front wall down. The oven was in!

When the first restaurant opened it sold pizza in slices and there were only a few tables. As in traditional Italian pizzerias, the idea was that you bought your pizza, then ate it standing up or took it away with you. Peter also remembered one of the great pieces of advice he'd been given: Italian pizzerias always offer free pizza when they first open, so he did too and the Soho-ites loved it. The oven from Rome and its operator worked long hours to meet the demand.

As with any business starting out, Peter's restaurant evolved, following advice from close friends and customers. From eating pizza off a piece of greaseproof paper, things soon moved on to offering paper plates and plastic cutlery (which sometimes melted in the hot cheese!), then finally to real cutlery and crockery. Peter realised that the London customers wanted to sit down, so he invested in more tables with the finest marble tops. He even changed the shape of the pizzas, deciding that round was the way to go. PizzaExpress was new, exciting, cool and totally different to anything Londoners had seen before. Queues started to form.

In 1967, restaurant number two opened in Coptic Street, Bloomsbury, and was an instant success. Peter employed fashionable Italian restaurant designer Enzo Apicella to bring his individual look and feel to the new premises and held an extravagant opening party – Peter liked a party! Located in an area of London that had few other restaurants at the time, the place soon flourished, and the unique interior with its cool,

attractively tiled look and vibrant colours won high praise. The 'loud' atmosphere that was part of the appeal was due to the sparse design and use of hard surfaces, still a feature of many PizzaExpress restaurants today. Ironically, Enzo Apicella's deafness meant he was unaware of this innovation being a benefit!

Locals appreciated the new lunch venue and there were always flocks of hungry tourists passing by en route to the nearby British Museum. This was also the restaurant where PizzaExpress began its long association with live music, with performances by the Original String Quartet.

Many more restaurants opened up in London and all over the UK, but each one had something special and individual about it, whether in the building or the design. Peter never saw himself as creating a chain; he called his restaurants 'a necklace of individual gems'. The paper plates may have been consigned to history, but the fresh ingredients and lively surroundings are a constant and remain a key part of Peter's pizza legacy.

It was a sad day in 2018 when we heard the news that Peter Boizot had died, aged 89. But his dream, personality and passion live on, as they have done since he sold the business in 1993. Times change, people change, fashions change, but one thing remains constant: pizza.

Looking to the future, we at PizzaExpress take inspiration from Peter's pioneering spirit and keep that alive today. We're passionate about what we do and proud of using the best ingredients to make perfect pizzas, so we want to share that with you. In the following pages, you'll find our secrets to successful dough-making, our favourite topping recipes, plus all the little extras such as salads, dressings and sauces – everything you need to know to make amazing pizzas in your own kitchen.

PIZZA INGREDIENTS

At PizzaExpress we are very particular about the quality of the ingredients that go into our pizzas. We want to share some information with you to help you source the best items, but first we want to tell you the story of our passata, which has been made to the same recipe and by the same producer in Italy for well over three decades.

OUR PASSATA

Passata is a beautiful mix of ripe tomatoes that have been sieved to remove skin and seeds, and then puréed. This story starts one day in 1987 when Peter Boizot, founder of PizzaExpress, was in Italy, looking to find the best supplier of passata for the pizzerias. He'd already been to see several companies and, on the advice of a friend, decided to visit the Grecis in Parma. Peter arrived at about 4pm and took part in trials with the chef in the Greci professional kitchen, tasting different tomatoes and combinations. Signor Gilberto Greci was there and they all stayed until late that evening to find exactly the right recipe for the PizzaExpress passata. A deal was done and the first contract signed for supplies to begin with the next tomato crop. It was the beginning of a relationship that continues to this day.

So what makes this passata so special? First, Greci make our passata in Parma, the heart of Italy's most famous food-growing region, and from every window you can see fields of beautiful produce. Second, the tomatoes used are 100 per cent Italian. In February of each year, agronomists meet with the farmers to draw up plans for the next planting. Fields are identified and the pulpiest and most flavourful tomato varieties chosen for seeding – varieties that best suit the local soil and the climate. The seasons are respected and the harvesting of the tomatoes begins only when they are perfectly ripe. This takes place from late July to early September and it is truly magical to watch the trucks come in, groaning with tons and tons of vibrant red tomatoes destined to become passata. The tomatoes are processed within twelve hours of being picked and enter the production process only after the quality of the harvest has been carefully checked to make sure it meets the rigorous standards of PizzaExpress.

As a finishing touch, fresh basil leaves are added, by hand, to each tin. The tin is then pasteurised, without the need of chemical additives or preservatives, to maintain the stability of the product. Signor Gilberto Greci has long since retired, but from time to time he will pop in when they are making our passata to give it a quick taste and ensure it is just as good as it was that day more than thirty-four years ago.

We love our passata and we know it is very special, but there are plenty of great brands, available in jars and cartons, in the shops, so try a few and use the best you can find.

ANCHOVIES

We use brown anchovies, rather than white, on our pizzas, as they add bags of flavour and cook to an almost melting consistency. You can buy them packed in oil in tins or jars.

White anchovies are salted for a much shorter time than the brown and then marinated in vinegar and oil, which gives them a sweet flavour and keeps the flesh firmer. They are best used in salads, for topping a bruschetta, or on their own as part of an antipasto.

CHEESE

As you will see in the recipes, we use a number of different cheeses, but the ones that come up most often are mozzarella and Parmesan.

Mozzarella: True mozzarella is made from the milk of water buffaloes and is called *mozzarella di bufala*. It is a fresh cheese with a beautiful creamy texture and usually comes packed in whey in a plastic bag or pot to keep it moist. It's wonderful in a salad, as a finish on a cooked pizza, or as the star of the show (such as on our Margherita Bufala). When you do use this cheese on pizza, it's important to drain it really well so the topping doesn't become too soggy.

Generally, though, we find that mozzarella made from cow's milk, known as *fior de latte*, is best for topping pizzas. It has a drier, chewier texture than buffalo mozzarella and comes in blocks, so is easy to dice. It's available in supermarkets and sometimes labelled 'pizza mozzarella'.

Parmesan: Parmesan is an Italian hard cheese that adds a wonderful salty hit and lots of extra taste to any dish. Grating it ensures an even coverage, while adding shavings as a finish on a cooked pizza gives a lovely texture as well as bursts of great flavour.

Proper Parmigiano-Reggiano is made only in certain provinces of northern Italy: Parma, Reggio Emilia, Modena and Mantua. Production follows traditional methods and is very strictly controlled. Producers must be inspected by the Parmesan Consortium and given their seal of approval. Grana Padano is a similar hard cheese, made in different areas of Italy, and can be used instead of Parmigiano-Reggiano.

We use Parmesan on all our pizzas that contain meat, but not on veggie pizzas because it is made with animal rennet. We source a special vegetarian cheese called Gran Milano for our restaurants, but if you want a veggie cheese to use at home, you will find Italian hard cheeses in supermarkets that are suitable for vegetarians.

Vegan cheese: You can also now buy a range of vegan cheeses, including mozzarella-style and parmesan-style products.

FLOUR

White: For our dough we generally use plain white flour, which gives a slightly chewy texture to the base and is a great all-rounder. It's available in every supermarket and good to have in your store cupboard. You could also choose a strong white or 'oo' flour, but this contains a higher level of protein and gluten, so will make your base more bready in texture.

Wholemeal: Wholemeal flour contains the whole grain, so has a higher level of minerals and dietary fibre, and gives a nuttier, earthier flavour than white flour. If used on its own, it makes a heavier dough, so it's best mixed with plain flour to get the best of both worlds in terms of flavour and texture.

Gluten-free: Gluten-free flour can be made from a variety of ingredients, such as rice, chickpeas, potato starch or tapioca. Our favourite for pizza dough is rice flour, as it has a good flavour and its texture makes it particularly good for flouring a surface when you are rolling out your pizza base. Have a look at our gluten-free pizza dough recipe on page 23.

MEAT

Pork is the mainstay of the pizzeria and is generally used in the form of ingredients that are already infused with flavour – they do the work for you. These are some of our favourites.

Calabrese and 'nduja sausage: Both originate from Calabria in southern Italy, and it is the Calabrian chillies that make them sing. Calabrese is a more traditional sausage that is best used thickly cut. If you can't find Calabrese sausage, a salami with chilli and a good blend of fat and meat makes a good alternative. 'Nduja is called a sausage but it is really a paste that can be spread. It's become hugely popular in the UK and is readily available in supermarkets and delis, usually in jars. When cooked, it oozes deep red oil, which carries the chilli heat around your pizza.

Cured and smoked meats: Pancetta and Parma ham add a deep salty flavour to dishes. Pancetta is cooked on the pizza, and we usually use thin slices that crisp up nicely in the oven. Parma ham, or prosciutto, is available in packets or freshly sliced from delis and is best applied as a cold finish to a pizza or enjoyed as an antipasto. Speck is a type of ham but has a different curing and smoking process. On our Al Tirolo pizza (see page 196) we add speck halfway through the cooking time.

Pepperoni: Packed with paprika and smoky goodness, this is readily available in supermarkets. We use a Hungarian Gyulai for the best flavour, but use whatever you prefer or can find. We like a sausage with a small diameter, so that the edges curve up in the heat and become little cups of flavour. Just make sure you place the slices on the very top of your pizza so that they get lovely and crisp.

MUSHROOMS

At PizzaExpress we love our mushrooms on bruschetta and pizzas, and in pasta. They add so much flavour to a recipe.

Fresh mushrooms: Portobello have a lovely meaty texture; chestnut have a characteristic earthiness and nuttiness; while closed cup or button mushrooms have a slightly milder flavour that's a good foil for the big hitters such as truffle oil. All are delicious and can be used interchangeably, depending on what you have available.

Dried mushrooms: Porcini and other dried mushrooms have to be soaked in warm water for 10–15 minutes to soften them before use. They impart rich flavour and make everything taste 'a bit more mushroomy'! The soaking water they leave behind is full of flavour too, so great to use in risottos. Be sure to pass the liquid through a sieve, as it can be a bit gritty from the mushrooms.

Truffles: These are the royalty of the fungi world and hugely expensive. But you can add a dash of their wonderful flavour by using truffle oil – olive oil infused with truffle.

OILS

Oils are an important part of our kitchen, in both cooking and finishing dishes. Extra virgin olive oil is often the best choice for finishing your pizza, adding a fruity, slightly peppery flavour that makes other ingredients shine. Garlic oil can be a great flavour shortcut. You can buy garlic-infused oil or make your own version for a more intense flavour.

Chilli oil is also great if you want some extra heat and glisten on your pizza. Again, you can buy it or try making your own by simply adding a few teaspoons of dried chilli flakes to extra virgin olive oil, and leaving it for a day or two. The oil will take on the red hue of the chillies, and the more you add, the hotter it will be!

ROASTED AND CHARGRILLED VEGETABLES

Roasted peppers, chargrilled artichoke quarters and chargrilled aubergines from a jar are full of deep smoky flavours and great to have on hand for pizza toppings. You can also buy them in tubs at deli counters. Sunblush tomatoes are also perfect for finishing pizzas.

You can, of course, prepare your own roasted or chargrilled veg. Just make sure you get an intense lick of flames and use plenty of olive oil and seasoning. Also, take a look at our recipes for various roasted veg on pages 245–247.

PEPPERS

Whether you like your peppers seriously hot, sweet or a bit milder, you can find something to suit you. There are more than 200 varieties of chilli pepper, and a good range is available in supermarkets, online and in ethnic stores. Their heat is measured by a special scale developed by Wilbur Scoville in 1912 and named after him; this heat scale is often noted on packs of chillies. You can buy chillies fresh, dried or preserved in oil. Dried chillies are available as flakes or powder.

Fresh chillies: Red or green, they always add a lovely zing, but if you prefer a milder heat, remove the seeds and membrane first. As a general rule, the larger the pepper, the milder the taste. Watch out for the really small bird's-eye chillies, as they are hot, hot, hot.

Preserved chillies: Great store cupboard items, these are available in jars and tins. Varieties to look for are hot green peppers (such as jalapeños), red chilli peppers and sweet picante peppers. You may also like chipotle peppers, which are dried, and smoked jalapeños. Little red chilli pepper pearls are also available in jars and are best on a salad or added to pizza after cooking. Their vibrant colour and hot, sweet flavour add another dimension to a dish.

TWELVE TOP TIPS FOR PERFECT PIZZA

1 Give your dough some love. Knead it well and give it time to prove. Some of our dough recipes, such as dough balls and garlic bread with mozzarella, need a second prove to ensure a light, fluffy inside and lovely crust with just the right level of chew.

2 When shaping or rolling out the dough, make sure it remains an even thickness.

3 Watch out for air trapped under the base – it can cause bubbles to form.

4 Most of the recipes are for Classic pizzas, but we've noted the additional quantities you need if you prefer to make Romanas. We've also included recipes for Calzones (folded pizzas) and for our Calabrese (rectangular pizza). And, if you like, you can divide your dough into four pieces instead of two and make small pizzas ('pizzette').

5 Make sure you preheat your oven so it's really hot when you pop in your pizzas.

6 Follow our guidelines and don't be tempted to overload your pizzas. All the toppings taste fantastic and we know just the right amounts to get the perfect balance of flavours. Too much of any liquid, for example, can make your pizza soggy.

7 When making pizzas that don't feature cheese in the topping, we add a little more passata than usual to keep the pizza moist.

8 The recipes all make two pizzas. When adding your toppings, be sure to divide the ingredients equally between the pizzas and distribute them evenly over the bases.

9 When dicing mozzarella and other cheeses, try to keep the pieces a similar size so that they melt evenly.

10 When adding slow-cooked meats, pull apart any large chunks.

11 When adding seasoning, be sure to season the whole pizza. And note that we don't use salt in our recipes. The hit of salt that's needed comes from the cheese and other ingredients.

12 We nearly always add black pepper to our pizzas, and we like to add a particularly generous amount to our mushroom pizzas.

MAKING DOUGH

We've had a few years (decades, in fact!) to get this right, and we are passionate about good dough, so we want to share what we've learnt with you.

The basis of our menu – dough – contains yeast, a living thing that needs to be looked after and nurtured to ensure you get the best results. In our pizzerias, we serve only perfect dough (as you would expect), so we always make sure it is proved correctly and looks just right. And you can do it too. At home, be sure to give your dough the time it needs to prove, and check that it has doubled in size and the surface looks beautifully smooth. Then you'll be ready to make all of our favourite recipes.

The volume of dough that's needed is too much for each pizzeria to prepare every day, so we make it all at our bakery in Oxfordshire. Here, our small team of bakers are dedicated to preparing our three types of dough: traditional, wholemeal and gluten-free. The dough is then sent out to our pizzerias to turn into great pizzas. They really know their dough at the bakery, and in the summer months they often give our restaurant managers and support teams a tour to show them where the pizza magic starts.

Then it's on to the business of making great pizza! If you like your pizzas light and fluffy, with a good crusty edge to dunk into one of our dips, our 1965 original Classic base is the one for you. The best technique for this one is to use your fingers to push and press the dough into shape, instead of using a rolling pin, as you want to keep in all the air that the yeast has worked so hard to develop. If you prefer a larger but super-thin base, Romana is the one to choose. For this, you do need to use a rolling pin to make the base really thin. There's no crusty edge, but that means more surface area for yummy toppings.

We've made most of the recipes in this book for the Classic base, but for each one we've listed the extra quantities you need if you decide to make a Romana. The choice is yours.

There's also our rectangular Calabrese to try when you fancy a change (see page 132) and the folded Calzone (see pages 95 and 142). Calzone is a pizza with a difference – the toppings are on the inside – and it makes a fabulously indulgent treat. All of our recipes can be cooked as calzones, but make sure not to use too many wet ingredients or the dough can become soggy.

For days when you want something lighter (but you also *really* want pizza), there's the Leggera – the pizza with the hole in the middle, filled with delicious salad. And for those who can't eat gluten, we have a gluten-free base. We want you to love it, so our bakers make sure this is just as great as the rest of our dough.

With this recipe, you can make our great PizzaExpress dough at home. It's really easy, even if you've never made bread or any sort of dough before. Just make sure you knead the dough well – don't be tempted to rush this stage – and allow time for it to double in size, or prove.

PizzaExpress Dough

MAKES I QUANTITY OF PIZZA
DOUGH (2 DOUGH PUCKS),
ENOUGH FOR 2 CLASSIC
OR ROMANA PIZZA
150ml warm water (about 27°C)
1 tsp caster sugar
2 level tsp dried yeast
    or 15g fresh yeast
225g plain flour, plus
    extra for dusting
1½ tsp salt
2 tbsp extra virgin olive oil

1. Pour the warm water into a bowl and add the sugar. Stir in the dried yeast, if using, or crumble fresh yeast into the water. Mix until the yeast has dissolved, then cover. Leave the mixture to stand in a warm place for about 15 minutes until a froth has developed on the surface – a sunny windowsill is ideal.

2. Sift the flour into a large mixing bowl, stir in the salt and make a well in the middle.

3. When the yeast is ready, add the olive oil, then pour the mixture into the well and stir.

4. Lightly flour your hands and slowly mix the ingredients by hand until they come together.

5. Generously dust your work surface with flour. Tip the dough onto the work surface and knead for 10 minutes until it's smooth and silky and no longer sticking to your fingers. Make sure you have enough flour on your work surface to stop the dough being sticky, but not so much that it becomes dry.

6. Divide the dough into two pieces. Very lightly oil your hands and shape the dough into two neat portions – often referred to as pucks. The oil from your hands will leave a very fine layer of oil on the dough pucks and will stop them drying out.

7. Put the dough pucks in separate bowls, cover with cling film or a tea towel and leave in a warm place until doubled in size. This will take 45–60 minutes, depending on the temperature.

Preparing Classic Pizza Bases

Do not use a rolling pin for shaping your Classic base. Rolling will remove the air that the dough has worked so hard to develop while proving and your pizzas won't have that characteristic PizzaExpress crust.

2 PizzaExpress dough pucks (see pages 18–19)
flour, for dusting
olive oil, for greasing

1. When the dough is ready, generously dust your work surface with flour and lightly oil a baking tray. Turn one piece of dough out onto the floured surface.

2. Press your fingers on the dough to flatten it until it has doubled in size. Turn the dough over and repeat. Keep pressing and pushing the dough into a circle with your hands, turning it regularly, until it measures about 24cm in diameter. You will see the rim of the dough rising as you work. Don't be tempted to use a rolling pin – our way works best, we promise!

3. Once your circle of dough is about 24cm in diameter, place it on the palm of one hand, then quickly pass it from one hand to the other to remove any excess flour.

4. Place the dough on the oiled baking tray. Repeat the steps with the other piece of dough, then you're ready to build your pizzas.

Preparing Romana Bases

The Romana base is larger and thinner than the Classic. It's OK to use a rolling pin for this one.

2 PizzaExpress dough pucks (see pages 18–19)
flour, for dusting
olive oil, for greasing

1. When the dough is ready, generously dust your work surface with flour and lightly oil a baking tray. Turn one piece of dough out onto the floured surface. Press your fingers on the dough to flatten it until it has doubled in size. Turn the dough over and repeat.

2. Using a rolling pin, roll out the dough into a circle measuring at least 30cm, depending on the size of your baking tray. At first, you will find that the dough springs back as you roll, but keep going and it will make the shape you want.

3. Once your circle of dough is about 30cm in diameter, place it on the palm of one hand, then quickly pass it from one hand to the other to remove any excess flour.

4. Place the dough on the oiled baking tray. Repeat the steps with the other piece of dough, then you're ready to build your pizzas.

Preparing Calabrese Bases

Just occasionally it's fun to make rectangular pizza. The base for our Calabrese recipe (see page 132) is rectangular in shape and slightly larger than a sheet of A4 paper.

2 PizzaExpress dough pucks (see pages 18–19)
flour, for dusting
olive oil, for greasing

1. When the dough is ready, generously dust your work surface with flour and lightly oil a rectangular baking tray. Turn a piece of dough out onto the floured surface.

2. Press your fingers on the dough to flatten it until it has doubled in size. Turn the dough over and repeat. Using a rolling pin, shape the dough into a rectangle measuring about 30 x 25cm. At first, you will find that the dough springs back as you roll, but keep going and it will make the shape you want.

3. When your dough is the right size, place it on the palm of one hand, then quickly pass it from one hand to the other to remove any excess flour.

4. Place the dough on the oiled baking tray and push out to cover the whole tray. Repeat the steps with the other piece of dough, then you're ready to build your pizzas.

This dough is slightly different to our regular and wholemeal recipes and is halfway between a batter and a dough. This quantity makes enough for two Classic pizzas with a thinner crust, similar to a Romana.

Gluten-Free Pizza Dough

MAKES ENOUGH
FOR 2 CLASSIC PIZZAS
200ml warm water
    (about 27°C)
2 tsp caster sugar
2 tsp dried yeast
    or 15g fresh yeast
200g gluten-free
    self-raising flour
1 tsp fine salt
2 tsp xanthan gum
2 tbsp olive oil, plus
    extra for greasing

1. Pour the warm water into a bowl and add the sugar. Stir in the dried yeast, if using, or crumble fresh yeast into the water. Mix until the yeast has dissolved, then cover. Leave the mixture to stand in a warm place for about 15 minutes until a froth has developed on the surface – a sunny windowsill is ideal.

2. Put the flour, salt and xanthan gum in a large mixing bowl and stir well. When the yeast is ready, add the olive oil, then pour the mixture into the bowl. Stir with a wooden spoon until the mixture is thick and well combined. It won't look like normal pizza dough because gluten-free dough needs to be wetter (but it will make great pizzas!).

3. Divide the dough into two portions – often referred to as pucks – and put them in separate lightly oiled bowls. Cover with cling film or a tea towel and leave in a warm place to double in size. This will take 45–60 minutes, depending on the temperature.

4. When the dough is ready, lightly oil a couple of non-stick baking trays and your hands. Place each dough puck on a baking tray and press and push it into a circle with your hands, turning it regularly, until it measures about 24cm in diameter. It's best not to use a rolling pin, as the dough tends to stick to it, but you could use a lightly oiled plastic bottle if you like. Then build and cook the Classic recipe of your choice in the usual way.

Our famous pizza with a hole! Less dough means fewer calories, so this one's great if you're watching your weight. We use wholemeal flour for our Leggera dough, but you can also use this recipe for Classic and Romana pizza – just double the quantities.

Leggera Pizza Dough

MAKES 1 QUANTITY
OF LEGGERA DOUGH
(1 PUCK), ENOUGH FOR
2 LEGGERA PIZZAS

100ml warm water
    (about 27°C)
½ tsp caster sugar
1 tsp dried yeast or
    8g fresh yeast
110g wholemeal flour,
    plus extra for dusting
¼ tsp salt
½ tbsp extra virgin
    olive oil, plus extra
    for greasing

1. Pour the warm water into a bowl and add the sugar. Stir in the dried yeast, if using, or crumble fresh yeast into the water. Mix until the yeast has dissolved, then cover. Leave the mixture to stand in a warm place for about 15 minutes until a froth has developed on the surface – a sunny windowsill is ideal.

2. Put the flour and salt in a large mixing bowl and make a well in the middle.When the yeast is ready, add the olive oil, then pour the mixture into the well and mix until the dough comes together but is still sticky.

3. Tip the dough onto a floured surface, then lightly flour your hands and form it into a ball. Knead the dough for 5 minutes or until smooth.

4. Very lightly oil your hands and shape the dough into a neat portion – often referred to as a puck. The oil from your hands will leave a very fine layer of oil on the dough puck and will stop it drying out.

5. Put the dough puck in an oiled bowl, cover with cling film or a tea towel and leave in a warm place until doubled in size. This will take 45–60 minutes, depending on the temperature.

Preparing Leggera Bases

1 Leggera dough puck (see page 24)
flour, for dusting
olive oil, for greasing

1. When the dough is ready, generously dust your work surface with flour and lightly oil a baking tray. Place the dough on the floured surface and divide in half.

2. Press your fingers on one piece of the dough to flatten it until it has doubled in size. Turn the dough over and repeat. Using a rolling pin, shape the dough into a circle about 24cm in diameter.

3. Place the dough on the oiled baking tray. Using a pastry cutter with a diameter of about 9cm, cut out the centre of the circle of dough.

4. Remove the centre circle. (You can discard this or make it into a small pizzette.) Repeat the steps with the other piece of dough, then you're ready to build your pizzas.

Use this dough to make our super-tasty dough balls, dough sticks, bruschetta and flatbread. You'll find a number of different toppings and ways of using these in the book – or make up your own!

PizzaExpress Bread Dough

MAKES 1 QUANTITY OF
BREAD DOUGH (1 PUCK)
75ml warm water (about 27°C)
½ tsp caster sugar
1 level tsp dried yeast
    or 7g fresh yeast
112g plain flour, plus
    extra for dusting
½ tsp salt
1 tbsp extra virgin
    olive oil

1. Pour the warm water into a bowl and add the sugar. Stir in the dried yeast, if using, or crumble fresh yeast into the water. Mix until the yeast has dissolved, then cover. Leave the mixture to stand in a warm place for about 15 minutes until a froth has developed on the surface – a sunny windowsill is ideal.

2. Sift the flour into a large mixing bowl, stir in the salt and make a well in the middle. When the yeast is ready, add the olive oil, then pour the mixture into the well and stir.

3. Lightly flour your hands and slowly mix the ingredients by hand until they come together.

4. Generously dust your work surface with flour, then tip out the dough. Knead the dough for about 10 minutes until it is smooth and silky and no longer sticking to your fingers.

5. Very lightly oil your hands and form the dough into a neat shape, known as a puck. The oil from your hands will leave a very fine layer of oil on the dough puck which will stop it drying out. Cover with cling film or a tea towel and leave in a warm place for about 45–60 minutes.

Preparing Dough Balls

These are fabulous served with our special garlic butter (see page 34), or you can make a sweet version (see page 236). Better still – make both!

MAKES 16 (SERVES 2)
1 quantity of bread dough (see page 26)
flour, for dusting
olive oil, for greasing

1. When the dough is ready, generously dust your work surface with flour and lightly oil a baking tray. Shape the dough into a tube and roll it back and forth until it is about 46cm long.

2. Cut this tube in half.

3. Keep cutting the pieces of dough in half until you have 16 even-sized slices.

4. Place these on the baking tray, cut side down, cover with cling film and leave to prove for 30 minutes. See page 34 for cooking instructions.

Preparing Garlic Bread/Bruschetta

You can add a variety of toppings (see pages 36–43) to garlic bread and bruschetta to make delicious starters or snacks.

MAKES 2
1 quantity of bread dough (see page 26)
flour, for dusting
olive oil, for greasing

1. When the dough is ready, generously dust your work surface with flour and lightly oil a baking tray. Divide the dough in half.

2. Shape each piece into a rough oval, about 15cm long and 10cm wide.

3. Tap off any excess flour, put the pieces of dough on the baking tray, then lightly brush them with olive oil.

4. Using a pizza slicer or a sharp knife, cut an 'S' shape in the centre of each piece of dough. Then cut another 'S' on either side, making 3 on each piece. The depth of the cuts doesn't matter, but make sure you don't cut right through at the ends. Leave the dough in a warm place to prove for at least 30 minutes.

Preparing Dough Sticks

The perfect accompaniment to our salads.

SERVES 2
1 quantity of bread dough (see page 26)
flour, for dusting
olive oil, for greasing
freshly ground black pepper

1. When the dough is ready, generously dust your work surface with flour and lightly oil a baking tray. Divide the dough in half and shape each piece into a rough oval, about 15cm long and 10cm wide.

2. Tap off any excess flour, put the pieces of dough on the baking tray, then lightly brush them with olive oil.

3. Using a pizza slicer or a sharp knife, cut an 'S' shape in the centre of each piece of dough. Cut another 'S' on either side, making 3 on each piece. The depth of the cuts doesn't matter, but make sure you don't cut right through at the ends. Leave the dough in a warm place to prove for at least 30 minutes. Preheat the oven to 230°C/Fan 210°C/Gas 8.

4. Once the dough has proved, cut right through the dough at the ends of the 'S' shapes, so the sticks can be separated once cooked. Season with black pepper and bake the dough sticks in the preheated oven for 6 minutes.

STARTERS

Memories with family and friends are what good times are all about, and food very often plays a central role in bringing people together. There's nothing nicer than sitting round a table in good company, enjoying a delicious meal. And nibbling on something tasty while you wait for your pizza is a great way to enhance that experience, whether it's sharing a plate of dough balls – and fighting over who gets the last one – or relishing a bowl of garlic prawns all to yourself.

The aim of a great starter is to tempt the appetite with flavourful morsels that delight without filling you up too much. Our bread dough forms the basis of quite a few of our favourite starters. It can be smothered in garlic butter and melted mozzarella, or topped with a fresh and zingy tomato bruschetta mix or our creamy mushrooms. Or if you fancy something lighter to save room for your main course, chicken wings or prawns make a great start to any meal.

Garlic bread and flatbread can also be served as sides – they're lovely with a salad or to dip into a juicy lasagne. If you'd like to add some salad leaves to your starters, you'll find all our dressing recipes on pages 244–45.

These delicious little morsels have been on our menu for more than thirty years. They're great served as a starter with some tasty garlic butter, or as a nice accompaniment to a salad or anything else you like. If you fancy a sweet version, try our snowball dough balls on page 236. Dessert heaven.

MAKES 16
1 quantity of bread dough
  (see page 26)
flour, for dusting
olive oil, for greasing

Garlic butter
4 tsp salted butter,
  room temperature
½ tsp finely chopped garlic

Dough Balls 'PizzaExpress'

1. When the dough is ready, generously dust your work surface with flour and lightly oil a baking tray. Shape the dough into a tube and roll it back and forth until it is about 46cm long.

2. Cut this tube in half, then keep cutting the pieces of dough in half until you have 16 even-sized slices. Place these on the baking tray, cover with cling film and leave to prove for 30 minutes. (For more info on preparing your dough balls for baking, see page 27.)

3. Preheat the oven to 230°C/Fan 210°C/Gas 8.

4. To make the garlic butter, mix the butter with the finely chopped garlic and set aside.

5. Bake the dough balls in the preheated oven for 6 minutes until golden and serve with the garlic butter.

One of our most popular and best-loved starters. Add more garlic if you dare – they do say it keeps vampires away!

MAKES 2
1 quantity of bread dough
    (see page 26)
60g block mozzarella, diced

Garlic butter
4 tsp salted butter,
    room temperature
½ tsp finely chopped garlic

To finish
a few parsley leaves

Garlic Bread with Mozzarella

1. Take your bread dough and follow the instructions on page 28 to prepare it for proving.

2. While your dough is proving, make the garlic butter by mixing the butter with the finely chopped garlic. You might have a bit more than you need, but the butter keeps well in the fridge for a few days and it's delicious on a baked potato.

3. Preheat the oven to 230°C/Fan 210°C/Gas 8.

4. Once the dough has proved, divide the mozzarella between the 2 pieces, spreading it evenly over the dough. Bake in the preheated oven for 6 minutes.

5. Remove the bread from the oven. Use a pastry brush to spread the garlic butter around the edges of each piece of bread, not over the cheese. Garnish with parsley leaves and serve at once.

MAKES 2
1 quantity of bread dough
    (see page 26)

Garlic butter
4 tsp salted butter,
    room temperature
½ tsp finely chopped garlic

Bruschetta mix
2 vine tomatoes, diced
½ red onion, peeled and diced
freshly ground black pepper

To finish
1 heaped tbsp pesto
    (see page 243 or
    shop-bought)
a few basil leaves

Bruschetta – toasted or baked bread with delicious toppings – is a very popular antipasto in northern Italy and dates back to the days when farm labourers would take a snack on some oiled, toasted bread to enjoy in the fields. Nowadays, the combination of garlicky bread, fresh tomatoes, pesto and basil leaves ensures this vibrant starter showcases the very best of Italian flavours.

Bruschetta Originale 'PizzaExpress'

1. Take your bread dough and follow the instructions on page 28 to prepare it for proving.

2. While your dough is proving, make the garlic butter by mixing the butter with the finely chopped garlic. You'll have a bit more than you need, but it keeps well in the fridge for a few days.

3. Preheat the oven to 230°C/Fan 210°C/Gas 8.

4. Mix the tomatoes and red onion for the bruschetta topping in a bowl and season with black pepper.

5. When the dough has finished proving, bake in the preheated oven for 6 minutes. Remove and spread with some garlic butter – a pastry brush is ideal for this. Divide the bruschetta mix between the pieces of bread and drizzle over some pesto. Garnish with a few basil leaves and serve.

This well-loved combination of mushrooms, béchamel sauce and red onion, served with bruschetta and finished with chopped parsley and balsamic syrup, has made regular appearances on our menu for many years. And judging by the excitement it generates, it'll continue to feature for a long time to come!

Bruschetta con Funghi

MAKES 2
1 quantity of bread dough
   (see page 26)
160g béchamel sauce
   (see page 242)
120g cup mushrooms,
   wiped and sliced
1 small red onion, peeled
   and finely sliced
freshly ground black pepper
1 tsp balsamic syrup
2 tsp chopped parsley

1. Take your bread dough and follow the instructions on page 28 to prepare it for proving.

2. While your dough is proving, prepare your mushroom topping. Make the béchamel sauce, then add the slices of mushroom and onion to the pan and cook on the hob for a few minutes. Season with black pepper and keep warm.

3. Preheat the oven to 230°C/Fan 210°C/Gas 8. When the dough has proved, bake it in the preheated oven for 6 minutes.

4. Place each piece of bread on a plate and spoon the mushroom mixture over one half of each piece. Drizzle with balsamic syrup, add a sprinkle of parsley, then serve.

MAKES 2
1 quantity of bread dough
   (see page 26)
3 tbsp passata
1 tsp garlic oil

Bruschetta mix
2 vine tomatoes, diced
½ red onion, peeled and diced
freshly ground black pepper

To finish
6 white anchovy fillets
1 heaped tsp capers
2 tsp chopped parsley
dessertspoon of chilli oil
2 lemon wedges

We use white anchovies for this, as they are are pickled in vinegar, or a mix of vinegar and oil, rather than salt, and have a milder, fresher, sweeter flavour than salted anchovies. They're generally eaten whole and don't need to be cooked, making them a perfect bruschetta topping.

Anchovy Bruschetta

1. Take your bread dough and follow the instructions on page 28 to prepare it for proving.

2. While your dough is proving, make the bruschetta mix. Combine the diced tomato and onion in a bowl, season with black pepper and stir well, then set aside.

3. Preheat the oven to 230°C/Fan 210°C/Gas 8.

4. Once the dough has proved, mix the passata with the garlic oil and spread it evenly over the pieces of dough. Bake for 6 minutes in the preheated oven.

5. Top with the bruschetta mix, then arrange 3 anchovy fillets on each bread. Sprinkle with capers and parsley, drizzle with chilli oil, then serve with lemon wedges on the side.

A delicious bread that began life on our vegan menu, this is so yummy that it's made it onto the main antipasti menu too. Fresh rosemary has an amazing aroma and taste, so is much better than dried here, but do take care to chop the leaves finely to distribute the flavour evenly over the bread.

MAKES 2
olive oil, for greasing
flour, for dusting
1 quantity of bread dough
    (see page 26)
1 dessertspoon garlic oil
1 tsp very finely chopped
    rosemary
freshly ground black pepper

To serve
60g houmous (ready-made)

Rosemary & Garlic Flatbread with Houmous

1. Preheat your oven to 230°C/Fan 210°C/Gas 8. Lightly oil a non-stick baking tray.

2. Lightly dust your work surface with flour. Divide the dough in half, then shape and roll each piece into a circle about 15cm in diameter – do not make raised edges around the dough. Place on the baking tray.

3. With a spoon, spread the garlic-infused oil over the flatbreads, taking it all the way to the edges. Sprinkle with rosemary and black pepper.

4. Using a pizza slicer or a sharp knife, create an 'S' shape across the centre of each piece of dough. Create another 'S' shape in the other direction to create 4 sections. Pierce the dough multiple times to prevent bubbles in the base which would burn.

5. Bake in the preheated oven for 6 minutes. Sprinkle the houmous with black pepper and serve with the warm bread.

12 chicken wings

Marinade
½ white onion, peeled
   and roughly chopped
3 garlic cloves, peeled
   and roughly chopped
2 tbsp olive oil
zest of 1 lemon and 1 tbsp
   lemon juice
½ tsp fennel seeds
½ tsp caster sugar
2 tsp salt
1 tsp chopped rosemary
1 tsp chopped thyme
pinch dried oregano
freshly ground black pepper

To finish
chopped parsley
60ml house dressing
   (see page 245)

A chicken wing has three parts: the tip, the middle section or wingette, and the drumette, which is the meatiest part and looks like a small drumstick. We use drumettes in our restaurants as we find they work best for this recipe, but the marinade is wonderful with whole wings or drumsticks too. These are so tasty, it's hard to stop eating them!

Lemon & Herb Chicken Wings

1. Put all the marinade ingredients in a food processor and process until smooth.

2. Place the chicken wings in a large bowl, add the marinade mix and stir well, so all the wings are nicely coated. Leave in the fridge for at least 2 hours.

3. Preheat the oven to 190°C/Fan 170°C/Gas 5. Place the marinated wings on a rack in a roasting tin and cook in the preheated oven for 40 minutes.

4. Garnish with chopped parsley and serve with the house dressing.

6 baby plum tomatoes, halved
60g roasted peppers
   from a jar, sliced
10 cooked or raw king prawns,
   peeled and deveined
40g salted butter,
   room temperature
1 garlic clove, finely chopped
2 tsp chopped parsley
2 pinches chilli flakes

Bruschetta mix
2 vine tomatoes, diced
½ red onion, diced
freshly ground black pepper

To finish
1 tbsp chopped parsley
8 dough balls (see page 34)
   or crusty bread

Pizzas are substantial, so this light, flavoursome dish makes an excellent starter – tickling your tastebuds without filling you up too much. You can buy many different types of prawn, but we like to use king prawns for this antipasto, as their meaty texture and good flavour stand up well to the strong tastes of garlic and chilli.

Garlic King Prawns

1. Preheat the oven to 200°C/Fan 180°C/Gas 6.

2. Put the tomatoes and peppers in an ovenproof dish and layer the king prawns on top. They should all fit quite snugly. Mix the butter and garlic to make a paste and dot this on top of the prawns. Sprinkle over the parsley and chilli flakes. Cook in the preheated oven for 10 minutes if using cooked prawns, or for 15 minutes if the prawns are raw, stirring halfway through the cooking time. Remove the dish from the oven and stir everything to combine.

3. While the prawns are cooking, make the bruschetta mix. Combine the diced tomato and onion in a bowl, season with black pepper and stir well.

4. Divide the prawn mixture between two warm serving dishes. Add the bruschetta mix on top and sprinkle with parsley to finish. Serve at once with dough balls or crusty bread.

Unlike the dough used for garlic bread and bruschetta, this recipe doesn't have a second proving time, so results in a flatbread with a generous crispy layer of golden cheese. It's perfect with salads, antipasti, soups and dips, but be warned – it's so delicious it doesn't last long!

MAKES 2
olive oil, for greasing
flour, for dusting
1 quantity of bread dough
   (see page 26)
2 tbsp grated vegetarian
   parmesan-style cheese
freshly ground black pepper

Antipasto Bread

1. Preheat your oven to 230°C/Fan 210°C/Gas 8. Lightly oil a non-stick baking tray.

2. Lightly dust your work surface with flour. Divide the dough in half and shape and roll each piece into a circle about 15cm in diameter. Place on the baking tray.

3. Brush the circles of dough lightly with oil and sprinkle the cheese evenly all over. Season with black pepper.

4. Starting from the edge, slice an 'S' shape all the way through each piece of dough. Repeat this another couple of times with even spacing. Make sure you slice all the way through the edge. You will end up with 6 sections.

5. Place in the preheated oven and bake for 6 minutes until golden brown. Best served warm, but delicious cold, too.

CLASSIC
PIZZA

In this chapter you'll find our classic recipes, the ones that over the years have formed the backbone of our menus, with some of them listed since day one. While it's fun to try something new, there are also times when you want something you know and love. For many people, our pizzas are hugely nostalgic and evoke great memories – a birthday treat, a work Christmas party or a first date, perhaps. The recipes have the quintessential flavours of PizzaExpress that have been part of so many wonderful occasions. We call these our 'classics', but they don't have to be made on our Classic bases. You can use the recipes to make Romanas if you prefer, or use a Leggera or gluten-free base. It's up to you.

Our passata, which you can read more about on page 8, plays an important role in this chapter, as many of the classic recipes have only a small number of toppings. The fewer the toppings, the more important it is for them to be super tasty, so make sure you use the best ingredients. A Margherita Bufala, for example, made with great dough, delicious passata and tomatoes, and the best buffalo mozzarella is a real treat.

Then there's the seasoning. Most of our pizzas are seasoned with fragrant oregano, the essential pizza herb, and some freshly ground black pepper. With these flavours, and a drizzle of olive oil or garlic oil, you can't go far wrong. We never add salt to our pizzas. Instead, a salty hit from ingredients such as delicious Parmesan cheese, crisp pancetta or anchovies does the hard work for us. And as Peter taught us over the years, mushrooms love black pepper, so always add a double pinch to any mushroom pizza.

We don't keep these recipes on our menu because it's easy or because that's what we have always done. They're there because they taste great and customers love them – we know that if we ever took the American Hot off the menu we would have a riot on our hands! Most of our classics are simple to make once you get the knack of preparing the dough, so give yourself a treat and make your very own PizzaExpress pizzas.

The Margherita pizza was created in 1889 for Queen Margherita, queen consort of Italy from 1878–1900, to mark her royal visit to Capodimonte, near Naples. Simple, yet utterly delicious, it's the foundation of almost every pizza you'd ever wish to make and has been on our menu since the very start.

Margherita

MAKES 2 CLASSIC PIZZAS
1 quantity of pizza dough
   (see pages 18–19)
olive oil, for greasing
   and drizzling
flour, for dusting
160g passata
140g block mozzarella, diced
2 pinches dried oregano
freshly ground black pepper

To finish
basil leaves

1. While your dough is rising, preheat your oven to 230°C/Fan 210°C/ Gas 8. Lightly oil a couple of non-stick baking trays.

2. Dust your work surface with flour. Press and push each piece of dough into a circle about 24cm in diameter. (For more info on working with your dough, see pages 20–21.) Place your pizza bases on the baking trays.

3. Using a tablespoon, spread a thin layer of passata over the pizza bases, taking it almost to the edges. Divide the mozzarella between the pizzas, making sure it is evenly distributed. Season all over with oregano and black pepper, then drizzle each pizza with about a teaspoon of olive oil.

4. Place the pizzas in the preheated oven and bake for 8–10 minutes. Garnish with basil leaves and serve at once.

ROMANA PIZZA
For 2 Romanas you'll need 180g mozzarella. The other ingredients stay the same.

Buffalo mozzarella is made from buffalo milk and is a beautifully soft, luxurious cheese that is perfect for pizzas such as this one, launched to mark our fiftieth birthday. Just make sure you drain the cheese well, so it doesn't make the pizza soggy. With most other recipes, a firmer mozzarella works best, so we generally use one made from cow's milk and known as *fior di latte*.

Margherita Bufala

MAKES 2 CLASSIC PIZZAS
1 quantity of pizza dough
    (see pages 18–19)
olive oil, for greasing flour,
    for dusting
160g passata
12 basil leaves
12 baby plum tomatoes, halved
1 x 125g ball of buffalo
    mozzarella, drained
4 pinches dried oregano
freshly ground black pepper
2 dessertspoons garlic olive oil

To finish
basil leaves
2 dessertspoons extra
    virgin olive oil

1. While your dough is rising, preheat your oven to 230°C/Fan 210°C/Gas 8. Lightly oil a couple of non-stick baking trays.

2. Dust your work surface with flour. Press and push each piece of dough into a circle about 24cm in diameter. (For more info on working with your dough, see pages 20–21.) Place your pizza bases on the baking trays.

3. Using a tablespoon, spread a thin layer of passata over the pizza bases, taking it almost to the edges. Add the basil leaves and tomato halves, dividing them equally between each pizza, then tear the mozzarella into pieces and distribute over the top. Season with oregano and black pepper and drizzle with the garlic oil.

4. Place the pizzas in the preheated oven and bake for 8–10 minutes. Garnish with basil leaves and drizzle with a little extra virgin olive oil, then serve.

ROMANA PIZZA
For 2 Romanas you'll need 2 x 125g balls of buffalo mozzarella. The other ingredients stay the same.

A simple but super-tasty pizza with the robust flavours of the different cheeses, this is heaven for cheese fanatics. Be sure to dice them all to about the same size so they cook evenly. We like to pop an olive in the centre so we can tell this pizza from a Margherita. You don't have to do this at home, but it does add a nice finishing touch. And if you'd like a piccante version of this pizza, drizzle over a couple of spoonfuls of sweet chilli jam before serving.

Quattro Formaggi

MAKES 2 CLASSIC PIZZAS
1 quantity of pizza dough
    (see pages 18–19)
olive oil, for greasing
flour, for dusting
160g passata
50g block mozzarella, diced
50g pecorino, diced
50g Italian blue cheese, diced
2 black olives, pitted
2 pinches dried oregano
freshly ground black pepper

To finish
20g vegetarian parmesan-style
    cheese, grated

1. While your dough is rising, preheat your oven to 230°C/Fan 210°C/Gas 8. Lightly oil a couple of non-stick baking trays.

2. Dust your work surface with flour. Press and push each piece of dough into a circle about 24cm in diameter. (For more info on working with your dough, see pages 20–21.) Place your pizza bases on the baking trays.

3. Using a tablespoon, spread a thin layer of passata over the pizza bases, taking it almost to the edges. Add the mozzarella, pecorino and blue cheese, dividing them evenly between the pizzas. Place an olive in the centre of each pizza and season with oregano and black pepper.

4. Place the pizzas in the preheated oven and bake for 8–10 minutes. Sprinkle over the grated cheese and serve.

ROMANA PIZZA
For 2 Romanas you'll need 80g mozzarella, 80g pecorino and 80g Italian blue cheese. The other ingredients stay the same.

One of our most popular vegetarian pizzas, the Padana is a feast of great tastes and textures. It's important to squeeze the spinach really well to get rid of excess water – you don't want a soggy-bottomed pizza – and be sure to distribute the chutney evenly for flavour perfection. Add the onion rings last, so they cook well and make the pizza look beautiful.

Padana

MAKES 2 CLASSIC PIZZAS
1 quantity of pizza dough (see
    pages 18–19)
olive oil, for greasing
75–100g spinach
flour, for dusting
160g passata
70g block mozzarella, diced
70g goat's cheese
60g red onion chutney
small red onion, peeled and
    thinly sliced into rings
2 pinches dried oregano
freshly ground black pepper
2 tsp garlic oil

1. While your dough is rising, preheat your oven to 230°C/Fan 210°C/ Gas 8. Lightly oil a couple of non-stick baking trays.

2. Wash the spinach and trim off any tough woody stems. Put the spinach in a pan with any water clinging to the leaves and cook briefly until wilted. Tip it into a colander placed over a bowl or sink and use the back of a wooden spoon to squeeze out as much water as you can. Set aside until ready to use.

3. Dust your work surface with flour. Press and push each piece of dough into a circle about 24cm in diameter. (For more info on working with your dough, see pages 20–21.) Place your pizza bases on the baking trays.

4. Using a tablespoon, spread a thin layer of passata over the pizza bases, taking it almost to the edges. Divide the mozzarella between the pizzas, making sure it is evenly distributed, then crumble over pieces of goat's cheese. Dot the chutney over the pizzas, then give the spinach a final squeeze and add little pinches of that as well. Lay rings of red onion over the top. Season with oregano and black pepper, then drizzle over the garlic oil.

5. Place the pizzas in the preheated oven and bake for 8–10 minutes, then serve.

ROMANA PIZZA
For 2 Romana pizza you need 90g mozzarella and 80g chutney. The other ingredients stay the same.

1 quantity of pizza dough
    (see pages 18–19)
olive oil, for greasing
    and drizzling
flour, for dusting
160g passata
12 black olives, pitted
2 slices (about 60g) ham
40g cup mushrooms,
    wiped and thinly sliced
130g block mozzarella, diced
2 pinches dried oregano
freshly ground black pepper

The name of this popular pizza translates as 'The Queen' and, sure enough, with a combination of black olives, juicy ham and mushrooms, it does have a selection of tasty ingredients fit for the most regal of pizza lovers!

La Reine

1. While your dough is rising, preheat your oven to 230°C/Fan 210°C/Gas 8. Lightly oil a couple of non-stick baking trays.

2. Dust your work surface with flour. Press and push each piece of dough into a circle about 24cm in diameter. (For more info on working with your dough, see pages 20–21.) Place your pizza bases on the baking trays.

3. Using a tablespoon, spread a thin layer of passata over the pizza bases, taking it almost to the edges. Arrange 6 olives around the edge of each pizza. Tear the ham into pieces and add these to the pizzas, then scatter over slices of mushroom. Divide the mozzarella between the pizzas, making sure it is evenly distributed. Season with oregano and black pepper, then drizzle each pizza with about a teaspoon of olive oil.

4. Place the pizzas in the preheated oven and bake for 8–10 minutes, then serve.

ROMANA PIZZA
For 2 Romanas you need 16 olives, 3 slices (90g) of ham and 170g mozzarella. The other ingredients stay the same.

1 quantity of pizza dough
    (see pages 18–19)
olive oil, for greasing
75–100g spinach
flour, for dusting
160g passata
12 black olives, pitted
130g block mozzarella, diced
2 pinches dried oregano
freshly ground black pepper
2 tsp garlic oil
2 free-range eggs

To finish
2 tbsp grated vegetarian
    parmesan-style cheese

We named this pizza after one of the most beautiful Italian cities, Florence, and we think it is more than worthy of the name. Even so, customers often forget and ask for 'the one with the egg'! Spinach and eggs are happy partners – think of eggs Florentine – so work perfectly combined on a pizza.

Fiorentina

1. While your dough is rising, preheat your oven to 230°C/Fan 210°C/Gas 8. Lightly oil a couple of non-stick baking trays.

2. Wash the spinach and trim off any tough woody stems. Put the spinach in a pan with any water clinging to the leaves and cook briefly until wilted. Tip into a colander placed over a bowl or sink and use the back of a wooden spoon to squeeze out as much water as you can. Set aside until ready to use.

3. Dust your work surface with flour. Press and push each piece of dough into a circle about 24cm in diameter. (For more info on working with your dough, see pages 20–21.) Place your pizza bases on the baking trays.

4. Using a tablespoon, spread a thin layer of passata over the pizza bases, taking it almost to the edges. Arrange 6 olives around the edge of each pizza. Leaving a space for the egg in the centre of the pizza, add small portions of spinach, then the mozzarella, distributing both evenly. Season with oregano and black pepper and drizzle a teaspoon of garlic oil over each pizza.

5. If you prefer your eggs cooked through, crack an egg into the centre of each pizza, place them in the preheated oven and bake for 8–10 minutes. If you prefer soft eggs, cook the pizzas for 4–5 minutes first, then add the eggs and cook for another 4–5 minutes. Sprinkle with grated cheese before serving.

ROMANA PIZZA
For 2 Romanas you need 16 olives and 170g mozzarella.
The other ingredients stay the same.

This pizza resulted from Peter's desire to keep the beautiful, yet threatened, city of Venice from falling into the lagoon! Today, donations from this pizza continue to go to the Venice in Peril Fund, and also, more recently, to the Nordoff Robbins music therapy charity. The recipe was inspired by a famous Italian fish dish which had a marinade made from onion, white wine vinegar, sugar, raisins and pine kernels.

Veneziana

MAKES 2 CLASSIC PIZZAS
1 quantity of pizza dough
(see pages 18–19)
olive oil, for greasing
and drizzling
flour, for dusting
160g passata
12 black olives, pitted
1 tsp pine kernels
1 heaped tbsp sultanas
1 tbsp capers
2 pinches dried oregano
freshly ground black pepper
small red onion, peeled and
thinly sliced into rings
130g block mozzarella, diced

1. While your dough is rising, preheat your oven to 230°C/Fan 210°C/ Gas 8. Lightly oil a couple of non-stick baking trays.

2. Dust your work surface with flour. Press and push each piece of dough into a circle about 24cm in diameter. (For more info on working with your dough, see pages 20–21.) Place your pizza bases on the baking trays.

3. Using a tablespoon, spread a thin layer of passata over the pizza bases, taking it almost to the edges. Place 6 olives round the edge of each pizza. Scatter over the pine kernels, sultanas and capers, dividing them between each pizza and spreading them evenly, then season with oregano and black pepper. Add the onion slices and the mozzarella, arranging them neatly over the top, then drizzle each pizza with a teaspoon of olive oil.

4. Place the pizzas in the preheated oven and bake for 8–10 minutes, then serve.

ROMANA PIZZA
For 2 Romanas you need 16 olives, 1 heaped tsp pine kernels, 1 heaped tbsp capers and 170g mozzarella. The other ingredients stay the same.

This is one of the oldest of all traditional pizza recipes and still much loved. Beautifully simple, it contains no cheese and is usually topped with anchovies, so if you're a fan, go for it and add four to your pizza. We've included instructions on how to make your own garlic oil for this recipe, but you can use shop-bought if you prefer.

MAKES 2 CLASSIC PIZZAS
1 quantity of pizza dough
    (see pages 18–19)
olive oil, for greasing
    and for the garlic oil
4 garlic cloves, peeled
    and very finely chopped
flour, for dusting
240g passata
4 pinches dried oregano

To finish
chopped parsley

Marinara

1. While your dough is rising, preheat your oven to 230°C/Fan 210°C/Gas 8. Lightly oil a couple of non-stick baking trays.

2. Make the garlic oil. Pour 20ml of olive oil into a bowl and stir in the finely chopped garlic. Set aside until needed.

3. Dust your work surface with flour. Press and push each piece of dough into a circle about 24cm in diameter. (For more info on working with your dough, see pages 20–21.) Place your pizza bases on the baking trays.

4. Using a tablespoon, spread a layer of passata over the pizza bases, taking it almost to the edges. Season all over with oregano, then drizzle each one with a dessertspoonful of garlic oil.

5. Place the pizzas in the preheated oven and bake for 8–10 minutes. Garnish with chopped parsley, then serve.

ROMANA PIZZA
For 2 Romanas the ingredients stay the same.

This PizzaExpress favourite is based on an American burger filling made of minced beef and lots of sauce and seasoning, known as sloppy joe. Lots of cooks claim to have invented it, including one named Joe, but we wanted our pizza to have an Italian-style name. This is so good, and if you have any leftover sloppy mix, you could make yourself some extra-tasty burgers too.

MAKES 2 CLASSIC PIZZAS
1 quantity of pizza dough
    (see pages 18–19)
200g sloppy mix
    (see page 248)
olive oil, for greasing
    and drizzling
flour, for dusting
160g passata
130g block mozzarella, diced
2 pinches dried oregano
freshly ground black pepper

Sloppy Giuseppe

1. While your dough is rising, make your sloppy mix (see page 248). Preheat your oven to 230°C/Fan 210°C/Gas 8. Lightly oil a couple of non-stick baking trays.

2. Dust your work surface with flour. Press and push each piece of dough into a circle about 24cm in diameter. (For more info on working with your dough, see pages 20–21.) Place your pizza bases on the baking trays.

3. Using a tablespoon, spread a thin layer of passata over the pizza bases, taking it almost to the edges. Dot small spoonfuls of sloppy mix evenly over the passata, then add the diced mozzarella. Season the pizzas all over with oregano and black pepper, then drizzle each one with about a teaspoon of olive oil.

4. Place the pizzas in the preheated oven and bake for 8–10 minutes, then serve.

ROMANA PIZZA
For 2 Romanas you need 170g mozzarella. The other ingredients stay the same.

The name means 'devil' and, sure enough, with a topping of spicy pepperoni sausage and hot green peppers, this is a pizza with attitude. Always add the Tabasco after cooking, to ensure an intense hit of heat.

Diavolo

MAKES 2 CLASSIC PIZZAS
1 quantity of pizza dough
(see pages 18–19)
150g sloppy mix
(see page 248)
olive oil, for greasing
and drizzling
flour, for dusting
160g passata
26 slices (50–55g) pepperoni
40g hot green peppers,
jalapeños or red chilli peppers
130g block mozzarella, diced
2 pinches dried oregano
freshly ground black pepper

To finish
Tabasco sauce, to taste

1. While your dough is rising, make your sloppy mix (see page 248). Preheat your oven to 230°C/Fan 210°C/Gas 8. Lightly oil a couple of non-stick baking trays.

2. Dust your work surface with flour. Press and push each piece of dough into a circle about 24cm in diameter. (For more info on working with your dough, see pages 20–21.) Place your pizza bases on the baking trays.

3. Using a tablespoon, spread a thin layer of passata over the pizza bases, taking it almost to the edges. Add the pepperoni, dividing the slices between the pizzas. Dot small spoonfuls of sloppy mix evenly over the passata, then add your chosen hot peppers. Divide the diced mozzarella between the pizzas and season with oregano and black pepper. Drizzle each one with about a teaspoon of olive oil.

4. Place the pizzas in the preheated oven and bake for 8–10 minutes. Finish with Tabasco sauce to taste, and serve.

ROMANA PIZZA
For 2 Romanas you need 170g mozzarella. The other ingredients stay the same.

1 quantity of pizza dough
    (see pages 18–19)
olive oil, for greasing
    and drizzling
flour, for dusting
160g passata
60g sweet picante peppers
    from a jar
150g cooked chicken
1 small red onion, peeled
    and thinly sliced into rings
130g block mozzarella, diced
2 pinches dried oregano
freshly ground black pepper
2 pinches Cajun spice
2 tsp garlic oil

Ad astra is a Latin phrase meaning 'to the stars'. The phrase has its origins with Virgil, who wrote in his Aeneid: *sic itur ad astra* (thus one journeys to the stars). A lovely thought and a delicious pizza – maybe the happy feeling it gives makes you reach for the stars!

Pollo ad Astra

1. While your dough is rising, preheat your oven to 230°C/Fan 210°C/Gas 8. Lightly oil a couple of non-stick baking trays.

2. Dust your work surface with flour. Press and push each piece of dough into a circle about 24cm in diameter. (For more info on working with your dough, see pages 20–21.) Place your pizza bases on the baking trays.

3. Using a tablespoon, spread a thin layer of passata over the pizza bases, taking it almost to the edges. Tear the peppers into pieces and add them to the pizzas – place them skin-side down so they don't burn. Tear the chicken into pieces and divide between the pizzas, then add the onion rings. Add the mozzarella and season with oregano and black pepper. Sprinkle the Cajun spice over the pieces of chicken to give great flavour and colour, then drizzle a teaspoon of garlic oil over each pizza.

4. Place the pizzas in the preheated oven and bake for 8–10 minutes, then serve.

ROMANA PIZZA
For 2 Romanas you'll need 170g mozzarella. The other ingredients stay the same.

This hot, spicy pizza has a mouth-watering topping of chilli peppers, chilli flakes and roasted mixed peppers, all combined with tender chicken. Power in the name and power in the flavour.

Pollo Forza

MAKES 2 CLASSIC PIZZAS
1 quantity of pizza dough
  (see pages 18–19)
olive oil, for greasing
flour, for dusting
160g passata
140g cooked chicken
60g roasted mixed peppers
  from a jar, sliced
40g red chilli peppers, sliced
130g block mozzarella, diced
2 tsp smoked chilli powder
freshly ground black pepper
2 pinches dried oregano
2 pinches chilli flakes
2 dessertspoons garlic oil

To finish
2 tsp chopped parsley
2 tbsp grated Parmesan cheese
2 dessertspoons chilli oil

1. While your dough is rising, preheat your oven to 230°C/Fan 210°C/Gas 8. Lightly oil a couple of non-stick baking trays.

2. Dust your work surface with flour. Press and push each piece of dough into a circle about 24cm in diameter. (For more info on working with your dough, see pages 20–21.) Place your pizza bases on the baking trays.

3. Using a tablespoon, spread a thin layer of passata over the pizza bases, taking it almost to the edges. Tear the chicken into pieces and spread it evenly over the pizzas. Add the roasted mixed peppers and the red chilli peppers, dividing them equally between the pizzas, then add the mozzarella. Sprinkle each pizza with smoked chilli powder and season with black pepper, oregano and chilli flakes. Drizzle a spoonful of garlic oil over each pizza.

4. Place the pizzas in the preheated oven and bake for 8–10 minutes. Remove from the oven, sprinkle with the parsley and grated cheese, then drizzle a spoonful of chilli oil over each one. Serve at once.

ROMANA PIZZA
For 2 Romanas you'll need 200g chicken, 60g red chilli peppers and 170g mozzarella. The other ingredients stay the same.

Purists do not recognise the addition of salami sausage on pizza, but we know we all love it. One of our first American customers, back in 1965, gave such a glowing description of his favourite pizza back home that our American was born. Laden with slices of fiery pepperoni, it has remained one of the most popular recipes on our menu.

American

MAKES 2 CLASSIC PIZZAS
1 quantity of pizza dough
    (see pages 18–19)
olive oil, for greasing
    and drizzling
flour, for dusting
160g passata
50 slices (about 100g) pepperoni
130g block mozzarella, diced
2 pinches dried oregano
freshly ground black pepper

1. While your dough is rising, preheat your oven to 230°C/Fan 210°C/ Gas 8. Lightly oil a couple of non-stick baking trays.

2. Dust your work surface with flour. Press and push each piece of dough into a circle about 24cm in diameter. (For more info on working with your dough, see pages 20–21.) Place your pizza bases on the baking trays.

3. Using a tablespoon, spread a thin layer of passata over the pizza bases, taking it almost to the edges. Add slices of pepperoni to each one, dividing them evenly, then add the mozzarella. Season all over with oregano and black pepper, then drizzle each one with about a teaspoon of olive oil.

4. Place the pizzas in the preheated oven and bake for 8–10 minutes, then serve.

ROMANA PIZZA
For 2 Romanas you'll need 60 slices (about 120g) pepperoni and 170g mozzarella. The other ingredients stay the same.

1 quantity of pizza dough
    (see pages 18–19)
olive oil, for greasing
    and drizzling
flour, for dusting
160g passata
50 slices (about 100g) pepperoni
40g hot green peppers,
    such as jalapeños,
    from a jar or tin, sliced
130g block mozzarella, diced
2 pinches dried oregano
freshly ground black pepper

Hot green chilli peppers from a jar or tin work best for this recipe. Fresh green chillies are fine too, but they won't give you that special tangy heat that people know and love about this hugely popular pizza.

American Hot

1. While your dough is rising, preheat your oven to 230°C/Fan 210°C/Gas 8. Lightly oil a couple of non-stick baking trays.

2. Dust your work surface with flour. Press and push each piece of dough into a circle about 24cm in diameter. (For more info on working with your dough, see pages 20–21.) Place your pizza bases on the baking trays.

3. Using a tablespoon, spread a thin layer of passata over the pizza bases, taking it almost to the edges. Add the pepperoni, dividing it evenly between the pizzas. Then add your choice of peppers and the mozzarella. Season all over with oregano and black pepper, then drizzle each one with about a teaspoon of olive oil.

4. Place the pizzas in the preheated oven and bake for 8–10 minutes, then serve.

ROMANA PIZZA
For 2 Romanas you'll need 60 slices (about 120g) pepperoni and 170g mozzarella. The other ingredients stay the same.

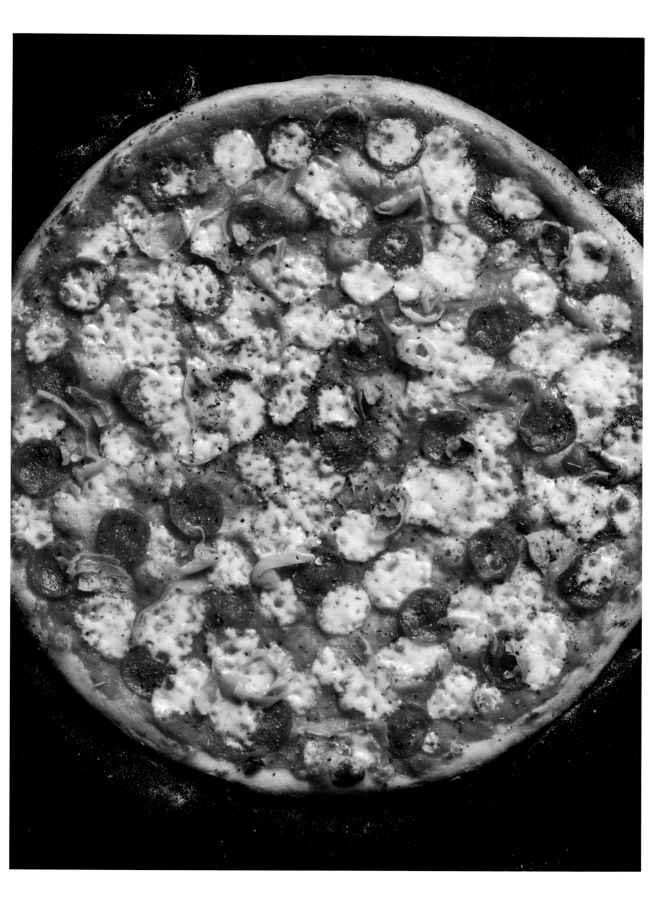

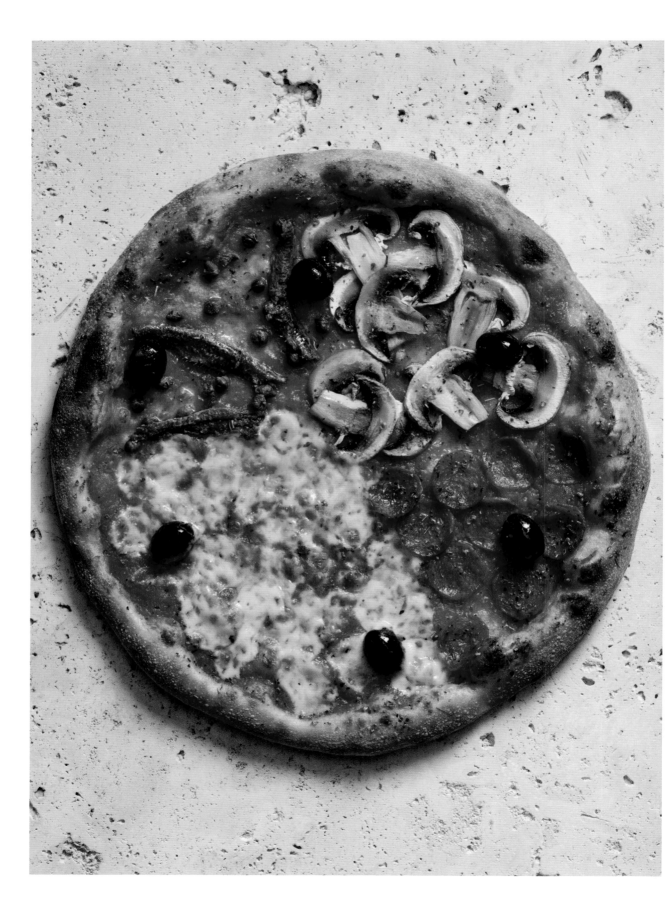

MAKES 2 CLASSIC PIZZAS
1 quantity of pizza dough
    (see pages 18–19)
olive oil, for greasing
    and drizzling
flour, for dusting
160g passata
12 black olives, pitted
40g cup mushrooms,
    wiped and sliced
20 slices (about 40g) pepperoni
60g block mozzarella, diced
1 heaped tbsp capers
6 brown anchovies
2 pinches dried oregano
freshly ground black pepper

This delicious combo pizza is a real crowd pleaser and has something for everyone. It's divided into four different sections, each with its own topping, but be careful not to get too carried away and overload it. If you like, reserve some dough and roll it out into thin strips to define the sections.

Four Seasons

1. While your dough is rising, preheat your oven to 230°C/Fan 210°C/Gas 8. Lightly oil a couple of non-stick baking trays.

2. Dust your work surface with flour. Press and push each piece of dough into a circle about 24cm in diameter. (For more info on working with your dough, see pages 20–21.) Place your pizza bases on the baking trays.

3. Using a tablespoon, spread a thin layer of passata over the pizza bases, taking it almost to the edges. Arrange 6 olives around the edge of each pizza. Add slices of mushroom to one quarter of each base, then pepperoni to another quarter. Add mozzarella to the quarter next to the pepperoni, then the capers and anchovies to the final section. Season all over with oregano and black pepper and drizzle each pizza with about a teaspoon of olive oil.

4. Place the pizzas in the preheated oven and bake for 8–10 minutes, then serve.

ROMANA PIZZA
For 2 Romanas you'll need 16 black olives, 50g mushrooms, 26 slices (about 50–55g) pepperoni and 80g mozzarella. The other ingredients stay the same.

VEGAN & VEGGIE PIZZA

Peter loved vegetarian pizza, so many of our original recipes were veggie and we often introduce new veggie ideas to the menu. In recent years, vegan pizzas have also become increasingly popular and we now have a dedicated vegan menu, as well as some vegan recipes on the main menu.

But how do you spot the difference? Once all the beautiful ingredients are baked together it can be difficult to tell some recipes apart. To solve this, our vegan pizzas have a special marker: half a baby tomato! This ensures that pizzas with dairy mozzarella can easily be differentiated from their vegan friends and helps both the team and the customers know exactly what's what.

We also use markers for other pizzas that can be easily confused. For our Quattro Formaggi, for example, we place a single black olive on the pizza so it doesn't get mistaken for a Margherita. Obviously, when you're making pizza at home this is not a problem, but in a busy pizzeria it's good to have these systems.

Do you sometimes think to yourself: I love that recipe but... In the restaurants, if you want a traditional recipe, such as the Verdure, but with vegan mozzarella, we're happy to make the switch (with the vegan marker, of course). And it works the other way too. If you love the Vegan Giardiniera but want regular mozzarella on your pizza, we can do it. Just remember your markers!

This favourite was our first vegan pizza to feature our delicious vegan mozzarella. The fresh, dairy-free alternative gives a perfect creamy balance to the pizza without overpowering the beautiful vegetables. This pizza also includes wonderful chargrilled artichokes from our amazing suppliers in Puglia, southern Italy. Grown with loving care, they are harvested in March, sliced into halves and quarters and chargrilled, then bottled in oil and garlic. You can taste the sunshine.

Vegan Giardiniera

MAKES 2 CLASSIC PIZZAS
1 quantity of pizza dough
   (see pages 18–19)
olive oil, for greasing
flour, for dusting
160g passata
1 small red onion,
   peeled and thinly sliced
60g cup mushrooms,
   wiped and sliced
8 chargrilled artichoke quarters
   from a jar (about 100g),
   torn into pieces
20 black olives, pitted
100g vegan mozzarella-style
   cheese, diced
2 pinches dried oregano
freshly ground black pepper
2 dessertspoons garlic oil

To finish
chopped parsley

1. While your dough is rising, preheat your oven to 230°C/Fan 210°C/Gas 8. Lightly oil a couple of non-stick baking trays.

2. Dust your work surface with flour. Press and push each piece of dough into a circle about 24cm in diameter. (For more info on working with your dough, see pages 20–21.) Place your pizza bases on the baking trays.

3. Using a tablespoon, spread a thin layer of passata over the pizza bases, taking it almost to the edges. Add the slices of onion, arranging them evenly over the pizzas, followed by the mushrooms and artichokes. Arrange 10 olives on each pizza and sprinkle over the vegan mozzarella. Season with oregano and black pepper, then drizzle a spoonful of garlic oil over each pizza.

4. Place the pizzas in the preheated oven and bake for 8–10 minutes. Garnish with chopped parsley, then serve.

ROMANA PIZZA
For 2 Romanas you'll need 24 black olives and 150g vegan mozzarella-style cheese. The other ingredients stay the same.

MAKES 2 CLASSIC PIZZAS
1 quantity of pizza dough
    (see pages 18–19)
olive oil, for greasing
flour, for dusting
240g passata
160g chargrilled aubergine
    slices from a jar
20g jalapeño peppers, sliced
20g red chilli peppers, sliced
40g smoky tomato harissa
    or regular harissa
2 pinches dried oregano
freshly ground black pepper
½ tsp smoky chilli powder
2 dessertspoons garlic oil

To finish
handful of rocket leaves
60g houmous (shop-bought)

In 2020 our customers voted the Vegan Mezze their favourite vegan Romana pizza, and it really does pack a punch of flavour. The blend of green jalapeños, red chillies, chilli powder and harissa give it a hot smoky taste hit that's balanced by the velvety roasted aubergine – no wonder customers keep on ordering this pizza. There's no cheese, but a finishing touch of houmous adds that essential creaminess.

Vegan Mezze

1. While your dough is rising, preheat your oven to 230°C/Fan 210°C/Gas 8. Lightly oil a couple of non-stick baking trays.

2. Dust your work surface with flour. Press and push each piece of dough into a circle about 24cm in diameter. (For more info on working with your dough, see pages 20–21.) Place your pizza bases on the baking trays.

3. Using a tablespoon, spread a layer of passata over the pizza bases, taking it almost to the edges. Since there is no cheese on this pizza, you need slightly more passata than usual to stop the base burning.

4. Add the chargrilled aubergine slices, dividing them evenly between the pizzas, followed by the jalapeños and chilli peppers. Add the harissa – about 10 or 12 little dollops per pizza. Season with oregano, black pepper and chilli powder, then drizzle each pizza with a spoonful of garlic oil.

5. Place the pizzas in the preheated oven and bake for 8–10 minutes. Remove them from the oven, sprinkle with rocket leaves, then add teaspoonfuls of houmous to each pizza before serving.

ROMANA PIZZA
For 2 Romanas you'll need 200g chargrilled aubergine slices and a large handful of rocket leaves. The other ingredients stay the same.

This is one of our oldest veggie pizza recipes and it's great as a regular pizza but it also works really well as a calzone. Our recipe is vegan, but if you want to add a little mozzarella, go for it and just use a little less of the other ingredients.

Calzone Verdure

MAKES 2 CALZONES
1 quantity of pizza dough
   (see pages 18–19)
olive oil, for greasing
75–100g spinach
flour, for dusting
160g Italian tomato dip
   (see page 243)
80g chargrilled aubergines,
   from a jar, chopped
80g roasted peppers
   from a jar, sliced
40g smoky tomato harissa
   or regular harissa
2 pinches smoked chilli powder
2 pinches dried oregano
freshly ground black pepper
2 dessertspoons garlic oil

Topping
olive oil, for brushing
2 pinches dried or finely
   chopped fresh rosemary

1. While your dough is rising, preheat your oven to 230°C/Fan 210°C/Gas 8. Lightly oil a couple of non-stick baking trays.

2. Wash the spinach and trim off any tough woody stems. Put the spinach in a pan with any water clinging to the leaves and cook briefly until wilted. Tip it into a colander placed over a bowl or sink and use the back of a wooden spoon to squeeze out as much water as you can. Set aside until ready to use.

3. Dust your work surface with flour. Press and push each piece of dough into a circle about 26cm in diameter – slightly larger than the Classic base. (For more info on working with your dough, see pages 20–21.) Place your pizza bases on the baking trays.

4. Using a tablespoon, spread a layer of tomato dip over half of each pizza base, leaving about 3cm around the edge. Add the aubergine and peppers on top of the tomato dip, then the spinach, dividing all the ingredients equally between the pizzas. Dot with harissa and sprinkle with chilli powder, then season with oregano and black pepper. Drizzle a spoonful of garlic oil over the filling in each pizza.

5. Using a pastry brush, brush a little chilled water around the edge of each base. Then fold the empty half of the calzone over the filling so the edges meet. Press along the edge of each calzone to seal together and crimp with your fingers. If you have a pastry crimper, run that around the edge and pull away any excess dough. Brush the pizzas with oil.

6. Season the calzones with rosemary and black pepper, then bake in the preheated oven for 8–10 minutes

MAKES 2 CLASSIC PIZZAS
1 quantity of pizza dough
   (see pages 18–19)
olive oil, for greasing
75–100g spinach
flour, for dusting
240g passata
2 pinches chilli flakes
60g cup mushrooms,
   wiped and sliced
8 chargrilled artichoke quarters
   from a jar (about 100g),
   torn into pieces
1½ tsp pine kernels
2 pinches dried oregano
freshly ground black pepper
2 dessertspoons garlic oil

To finish
chopped parsley
handful of rocket leaves
2 dessertspoons extra
   virgin olive oil

The Pianta was our first vegan pizza and contains no cheese. We add a bit more passata than usual to keep it moist and succulent. Like the Giardiniera, it features chargrilled artichokes, but this time they're joined by a sprinkling of pine kernels, cooked spinach and a generous seasoning of oregano, chilli flakes and garlic oil. Fresh parsley and peppery rocket give an extra boost of flavour and colour.

Pianta

1. While your dough is rising, preheat your oven to 230°C/Fan 210°C/Gas 8. Lightly oil a couple of non-stick baking trays.

2. Wash the spinach and trim off any tough woody stems. Put the spinach in a pan with any water clinging to the leaves and cook briefly until wilted. Tip it into a colander placed over a bowl or sink and use the back of a wooden spoon to squeeze out as much water as you can. Set aside until ready to use.

3. Dust your work surface with flour. Press and push each piece of dough into a circle about 24cm in diameter. (For more info on working with your dough, see pages 20–21.) Place your pizza bases on the baking trays.

4. Using a tablespoon, spread a layer of passata over the pizza bases, taking it almost to the edges, then sprinkle with chilli flakes. Add little dollops of spinach and the mushrooms and artichokes. Sprinkle over the pine kernels and season with oregano and black pepper. Drizzle a spoonful of garlic oil over each pizza.

5. Place the pizzas in the preheated oven and bake for 8–10 minutes. Sprinkle with chopped parsley and rocket leaves, then drizzle with the extra virgin olive oil and serve.

ROMANA PIZZA
For 2 Romanas you'll need 12 chargrilled artichoke quarters (about 150g) and a large handful of rocket leaves. The other ingredients stay the same.

1 quantity of pizza dough
   (see pages 18–19)
olive oil, for greasing
flour, for dusting
160g Italian tomato dip
   (see page 243) or passata
160g roasted vegetables
   (see page 245)
70g block mozzarella, diced
70g ricotta
2 pinches dried oregano
freshly ground black pepper
2 dessertspoons garlic oil

To finish
6 sunblush tomatoes
20g vegetarian parmesan-style
   cheese shavings

One of the secrets of successful veggie pizzas is to incorporate plenty of big flavours while making sure the topping isn't so wet that it causes a soggy base. Roasted or chargrilled veg, sunblush tomatoes, garlic oil and harissa are all key ingredients in our veggie range. For extra punch, we decided to use our Italian tomato dip (see page 243) instead of passata when we first launched this recipe, but it's fine to use passata if you prefer. If you do go the passata route, make sure you add some finely chopped garlic to it and include the delicious garlic oil to make this beautiful summery pizza sing!

Roasted Veg & Ricotta

1. While your dough is rising, preheat your oven to 230°C/Fan 210°C/Gas 8. Lightly oil a couple of non-stick baking trays.

2. Dust your work surface with flour. Press and push each piece of dough into a circle about 24cm in diameter. (For more info on working with your dough, see pages 20–21.) Place your pizza bases on the baking trays.

3. Using a tablespoon, spread a thin layer of Italian tomato dip or passata over the pizza bases, taking it almost to the edges. Add the roasted vegetables, then the mozzarella, dividing them equally between the pizzas. Then dollop teaspoons of ricotta over them both. Season with oregano and black pepper, then drizzle a spoonful of garlic oil over each pizza.

4. Place the pizzas in the preheated oven and bake for 8–10 minutes. Add the sunblush tomatoes and sprinkle with shavings of cheese, then serve at once.

ROMANA PIZZA
For 2 Romanas you'll need 240g roasted vegetables, 90g mozzarella, 100g ricotta, 12 sunblush tomatoes and 30g vegetarian parmesan-style cheese. The other ingredients stay the same.

This pizza was our Christmas 2019 vegan special. With a topping of spinach, peppers and potatoes, it is colourful and vibrant – a great combination of textures and flavours on a beautiful butternut squash base.

Vegan Zucca

MAKES 2 CLASSIC PIZZAS
1 quantity of pizza dough
    (see pages 18–19)
olive oil, for greasing
120g new potatoes, scrubbed
75–100g spinach
flour, for dusting
240g roasted butternut squash
    purée (see page 246)
2 pinches dried or finely
    chopped fresh rosemary
2 pinches dried or finely
    chopped fresh sage
60g sweet red peppers
    from a jar, torn into pieces
20ml balsamic dressing
    (see page 245)
freshly ground black pepper
1 tsp pine kernels
2 dessertspoons garlic oil

To finish
handful of rocket leaves
2 dessertspoons chilli oil

1. While your dough is rising, preheat your oven to 230°C/Fan 210°C/ Gas 8. Lightly oil a couple of non-stick baking trays.

2. Cook the potatoes in a pan of salted water until tender, then drain, slice thinly and set aside. Wash the spinach and trim off any tough woody stems. Put the spinach in a pan with any water clinging to the leaves and cook briefly until wilted. Tip it into a colander placed over a bowl or sink and use the back of a wooden spoon to squeeze out as much water as you can. Set aside until ready to use.

3. Dust your work surface with flour. Press and push each piece of dough into a circle about 24cm in diameter. (For more info on working with your dough, see pages 20–21.) Place your pizza bases on the baking trays.

4. Using a tablespoon, spread a thin layer of butternut squash purée over the pizza bases, taking it almost to the edges. Sprinkle over the rosemary and sage, then add the slices of potato. Add little dollops of spinach, arranging them evenly over the pizzas, followed by the sweet peppers.

5. Drizzle with balsamic dressing and season with pepper. Scatter over the pine kernels, then add a spoonful of garlic oil to each pizza.

6. Place the pizzas in the preheated oven and bake for 8–10 minutes. Garnish with rocket leaves, drizzle with chilli oil and serve.

ROMANA PIZZA
For 2 Romanas you'll need 40ml balsamic dressing, a heaped teaspoon of pine kernels and a large handful of rocket leaves. The other ingredients stay the same.

Courgettes (*zucchini* in Italian) are great ingredients for pizzas. In this recipe they are simply grated and added to the topping, but they can be chargrilled with other veg, or large slices can be used as bases for mini-pizzas, replacing the dough altogether! This is a beautiful white pizza – a bianca – made without tomato, but it has plenty of garlic oil, oregano and black pepper, plus red onion for colour and flavour. Be careful not to add too much cheese, as it shouldn't overpower the more delicate taste of the courgettes.

Zucchini

MAKES 2 CLASSIC PIZZAS
1 quantity of pizza dough
 (see pages 18–19)
olive oil, for greasing
flour, for dusting
100g béchamel sauce
 (see page 242)
100g courgettes, grated
1 small red onion, peeled
 and thinly sliced
130g block mozzarella, diced
30g vegetarian parmesan-style
 cheese, grated
2 pinches dried oregano
freshly ground black pepper
1 dessertspoon garlic oil

1. While your dough is rising, preheat your oven to 230°C/Fan 210°C/Gas 8. Lightly oil a couple of non-stick baking trays.

2. Dust your work surface with flour. Press and push each piece of dough into a circle about 24cm in diameter. (For more info on working with your dough, see pages 20–21.) Place your pizza bases on the baking trays.

3. Using a tablespoon, spread an even layer of béchamel over the pizza bases, taking it almost to the edges. Scatter over the grated courgettes and the onion slices, dividing them evenly between the pizzas. Add the mozzarella and sprinkle over the grated cheese. Season with oregano and black pepper, then finish with a drizzle of garlic oil.

4. Place the pizzas in the preheated oven and bake for 8–10 minutes.

ROMANA PIZZA
For 2 Romanas you'll need 160g béchamel sauce and 170g mozzarella. The other ingredients stay the same.

MAKES 2 CLASSIC PIZZAS
1 quantity of pizza dough
   (see pages 18–19)
olive oil, for greasing
flour, for dusting
160g passata
12 basil leaves
12 baby plum tomatoes, halved
130g block mozzarella, diced
2 pinches dried oregano
freshly ground black pepper
2 dessertspoons garlic oil

To finish
40g (2 heaped tbsp) pesto
   (see page 243 or shop-bought)

This is a twist on a classic favourite: the Margherita. It's a simple pizza but it's one of our best-sellers and authentically Italian – even its colours mirror those of the Italian flag. The topping of tomatoes, fragrant basil and creamy mozzarella, finished off with rich pesto, creates a heavenly combination of flavours.

Pomodoro Pesto

1. While your dough is rising, preheat your oven to 230°C/Fan 210°C/Gas 8. Lightly oil a couple of non-stick baking trays.

2. Dust your work surface with flour. Press and push each piece of dough into a circle about 24cm in diameter. (For more info on working with your dough, see pages 20–21.) Place your pizza bases on the baking trays.

3. Using a tablespoon, spread a thin layer of passata over the pizza bases, taking it almost to the edges. Tear the basil leaves and scatter them over the pizzas. Add the tomato halves, cut side up, dividing them evenly between the bases, then add the mozzarella. Season with oregano and black pepper and drizzle over the garlic oil.

4. Place the pizzas in the preheated oven and bake for 8–10 minutes. Spoon the pesto over the cooked pizzas, then serve.

ROMANA PIZZA
For 2 Romanas you'll need 170g mozzarella. The other ingredients stay the same.

The Soho is named after the central London neighbourhood where the first PizzaExpress restaurant opened in 1965. This pizza has the true hallmark of Italian cuisine – simplicity – and has been a great hit with customers since its first appearance on the menu in 2001. The classic flavour combo of passata, mozzarella and olives is topped off with plenty of peppery rocket leaves and shavings of cheese. Garlic is a key ingredient here, so don't miss out the garlic oil.

Soho

MAKES 2 CLASSIC PIZZAS
1 quantity of pizza dough (see pages 18–19)
olive oil, for greasing
flour, for dusting
160g passata
12 black olives, pitted
130g block mozzarella, diced
2 pinches dried oregano
freshly ground black pepper
2 dessertspoons garlic oil

To finish
large handful of rocket leaves
30g vegetarian parmesan-style cheese shavings
2 tsp extra virgin olive oil

1. While your dough is rising, preheat your oven to 230°C/Fan 210°C/Gas 8. Lightly oil a couple of non-stick baking trays.

2. Dust your work surface with flour. Press and push each piece of dough into a circle about 24cm in diameter. (For more info on working with your dough, see pages 20–21.) Place your pizza bases on the baking trays.

3. Using a tablespoon, spread a thin layer of passata over the pizza bases, taking it almost to the edges. Arrange 6 olives around the edge of each pizza. Spread the mozzarella evenly over the bases, then season with oregano and black pepper. Drizzle each pizza with a spoonful of garlic oil.

4. Place the pizzas in the preheated oven and bake for 8–10 minutes. Garnish with rocket leaves, sprinkle over the shavings of cheese, making sure you cover the whole of the pizzas. Drizzle with extra virgin olive oil before serving.

ROMANA PIZZA
For 2 Romanas you'll need 16 black olives, 170g mozzarella and a couple of handfuls of rocket leaves. The other ingredients stay the same.

The name of this pizza means wild mushrooms or forest mushrooms and certainly sounds more romantic and tempting than 'mushroom pizza'! The main topping ingredient is slices of succulent portobello mushrooms piled onto garlicky tomato dip. If you don't want to make the tomato dip, you can just add a couple of cloves of finely chopped garlic to regular passata, but you really do need that flavour hit. Mushrooms and garlic are the best of friends.

Funghi di Bosco

1. While your dough is rising, preheat your oven to 230°C/Fan 210°C/Gas 8. Lightly oil a couple of non-stick baking trays.

2. Dust your work surface with flour. Press and push each piece of dough into a circle about 24cm in diameter. (For more info on working with your dough, see pages 20–21.) Place your pizza bases on the baking trays.

3. Using a tablespoon, spread a thin layer of Italian tomato dip or passata over the pizza bases, taking it almost to the edges. Now add the mushroom slices, dividing them evenly between the pizzas. We like to arrange them beautifully, starting with a ring of slices around the edge, stalks facing in, and following the same pattern into the centre. Scatter the mozzarella over the pizzas, then season with rosemary and black pepper. Drizzle with the garlic oil.

4. Place the pizzas in the preheated oven and bake for 8–10 minutes. Add the shavings of cheese and sprinkle over the parsley, then serve.

ROMANA PIZZA
For 2 Romanas you'll need 240g portobello mushrooms, 170g mozzarella and 30g vegetarian parmesan-style cheese shavings. The other ingredients stay the same.

MAKES 2 CLASSIC PIZZAS
1 quantity of pizza dough
    (see pages 18–19)
olive oil, for greasing
flour, for dusting
160g Italian tomato dip
    (see page 243) or passata
160g portobello mushrooms,
    wiped and sliced
130g block mozzarella, diced
2 pinches dried or very finely
    chopped fresh rosemary
freshly ground black pepper
2 dessertspoons garlic oil

To finish
20g vegetarian parmesan-style
    cheese shavings
1 tbsp chopped parsley

1 quantity of pizza dough
(see pages 18–19)
olive oil, for greasing
flour, for dusting
100g béchamel sauce
(see page 242)
80g portobello mushrooms,
wiped and sliced
60g cup mushrooms,
wiped and sliced
50g ricotta
70g block mozzarella, diced
1 tsp dried or finely chopped
fresh rosemary
freshly ground black pepper
20g grated vegetarian
parmesan-style cheese
2 dessertspoons garlic oil

To finish
1 tbsp chopped parsley
20g grated vegetarian
parmesan-style cheese
2 dessertspoons truffle oil

We've noticed that truffle flavours have become increasingly popular, and a dash of truffle oil is an easy way to enrich the taste of a mushroom pizza. There's a good range of truffle oils available now; they're not cheap but the flavour is strong, so use the oil sparingly and think of it more as a seasoning. The slices of mushroom should almost cover the whole base of this pizza, with the cup mushrooms tucked in between the portobellos.

Mushroom & Truffle

1. While your dough is rising, preheat your oven to 230°C/Fan 210°C/Gas 8. Lightly oil a couple of non-stick baking trays.

2. Dust your work surface with flour. Press and push each piece of dough into a circle about 24cm in diameter. (For more info on working with your dough, see pages 20–21.) Place your pizza bases on the baking trays.

3. Using a tablespoon, spread a layer of béchamel over the pizza bases, taking it almost to the edges. Arrange the slices of portobello mushrooms over the pizzas, following the circular shape. Add the cup mushrooms in any gaps between the portobello slices.

4. Now, dollop ricotta onto the pizzas – about 5 teaspoons on each one – and scatter over the mozzarella. Season with rosemary and black pepper, then sprinkle over the grated cheese and drizzle each pizza with a spoonful of garlic oil.

5. Place the pizzas in the preheated oven and bake for 8–10 minutes. Sprinkle with the parsley and grated cheese, then drizzle with truffle oil before serving.

ROMANA PIZZA
For 2 Romanas you'll need 160g béchamel sauce, 120g portobello mushrooms, 80g cup mushrooms, 100g ricotta and 90g mozzarella. The other ingredients stay the same.

MAKES 2 CLASSIC PIZZAS
1 quantity of pizza dough
   (see pages 18–19)
olive oil, for greasing
flour, for dusting
120g passata
40g (2 heaped tbsp) pesto
   (see page 243 or
   shop-bought)
200g mixed Italian
   tomatoes, chopped
4 asparagus spears
130g block mozzarella, diced
2 pinches dried or chopped
   fresh thyme
freshly ground black pepper

To finish
2 tsp extra virgin olive oil
16 basil leaves

Another twist on our famous Margherita, this pizza has a mix of passata and pesto on the base and a generous topping of fresh tomatoes. We suggest you choose three or four different varieties of tomatoes, preferably in different colours to make your pizza look more exciting, and chop them all to a similar size. Pesto and asparagus spears add extra bursts of flavour.

Quattro Pomodoro

1. While your dough is rising, preheat your oven to 230°C/Fan 210°C/Gas 8. Lightly oil a couple of non-stick baking trays.

2. Dust your work surface with flour. Press and push each piece of dough into a circle about 24cm in diameter. (For more info on working with your dough, see pages 20–21.) Place your pizza bases on the baking trays.

3. Mix the passata and pesto together in a bowl to make our red pesto sauce. Using a tablespoon, spread a thin layer of the mixture over the pizza bases, taking it almost to the edges. Add the chopped tomatoes, arrange 2 asparagus spears on each pizza and scatter over the mozzarella. Season with thyme and black pepper.

4. Place the pizzas in the preheated oven and bake for 8–10 minutes. Then drizzle with the extra virgin olive oil and garnish with basil leaves.

ROMANA PIZZA
For 2 Romanas you'll need 300g mixed Italian tomatoes and 170g mozzarella. The other ingredients stay the same.

Artichokes, black olives, red onions, garlic oil and a scattering of parsley all feature in this flavourful pizza, named for the famous square in Rome. Campo de' Fiore means 'field of flowers', and the square is the site of a wonderful flower, fruit and vegetable market during the day. In springtime, stalls are piled high with beautiful fresh artichokes.

Campo de' Fiore

MAKES 2 CLASSIC PIZZAS
1 quantity of pizza dough
   (see pages 18–19)
olive oil, for greasing
flour, for dusting
160g passata
1 small red onion, peeled
   and thinly sliced
8 chargrilled artichoke quarters
   from a jar (about 100g),
   torn into pieces
12 black olives, pitted and halved
2 dessertspoons garlic oil
130g block mozzarella, diced
2 pinches dried oregano
freshly ground black pepper

To finish
1 tbsp chopped parsley

1. While your dough is rising, preheat your oven to 230°C/Fan 210°C/ Gas 8. Lightly oil a couple of non-stick baking trays.

2. Dust your work surface with flour. Press and push each piece of dough into a circle about 24cm in diameter. (For more info on working with your dough, see pages 20–21.) Place your pizza bases on the baking trays.

3. Using a tablespoon, spread a thin layer of passata over the pizza bases, taking it almost to the edges. Add the slices of onion and pieces of artichoke, spreading them evenly over the pizzas. Dot the olives over the top, then drizzle a spoonful of garlic oil over each pizza. Scatter over the mozzarella and season with oregano and black pepper.

4. Place the pizzas in the preheated oven and bake for 8–10 minutes. Finish with chopped parsley, then serve.

ROMANA PIZZA
For 2 Romanas you'll need 12 chargrilled artichoke quarters (about 150g), 16 olives and 170g mozzarella. The other ingredients stay the same.

Caponata is a much-loved Sicilian vegetable dish consisting of chunks of aubergine, fried in olive oil and mixed with tomatoes, capers, olives and chopped celery. The mixture is seasoned with wine vinegar and a touch of sugar to give a delicious sweet and sour flavour. It's one of those traditional recipes where every family has its own version, adding extra ingredients such as pine kernels, almonds, raisins – even bitter cocoa. The dish inspired us to use similar ingredients for this popular pizza topping.

Caponata

MAKES 2 CLASSIC PIZZAS
1 quantity of pizza dough
   (see pages 18–19)
olive oil, for greasing
flour, for dusting
160g passata
120g roasted aubergine
   (see page 246)
1 heaped tbsp sultanas
1 tbsp capers
1 tsp pine kernels
1 x 125g ball of buffalo
   mozzarella, drained
20g grated vegetarian
   parmesan-style cheese
2 pinches dried oregano
freshly ground black pepper

To finish
20g grated vegetarian
   parmesan-style cheese
10 basil leaves

1. While your dough is rising, preheat your oven to 230°C/Fan 210°C/Gas 8. Lightly oil a couple of non-stick baking trays.

2. Dust your work surface with flour. Press and push each piece of dough into a circle about 24cm in diameter. (For more info on working with your dough, see pages 20–21.) Place your pizza bases on the baking trays.

3. Using a tablespoon, spread a thin layer of passata over the pizza bases, taking it almost to the edges. Add the pieces of roasted aubergine, dividing them evenly between the pizzas, then sprinkle over the sultanas, capers and pine kernels. Tear the mozzarella into pieces and scatter them over the pizzas, then sprinkle over the grated cheese. Season with oregano and black pepper.

4. Place the pizzas in the preheated oven and bake for 8–10 minutes. Sprinkle with the grated cheese and garnish with basil leaves, then serve.

ROMANA PIZZA
For 2 Romanas you'll need 2 tsp vegetarian parmesan-style cheese for the pizzas, and 2 tsp more to finish. The other ingredients stay the same.

1 quantity of pizza dough
    (see pages 18–19)
olive oil, for greasing
flour, for dusting
160g passata
1 dessertspoon garlic oil,
    plus extra for drizzling
2 pinches chilli flakes
1 tsp chopped parsley
120g chargrilled aubergine slices
    from a jar, halved, or roasted
    aubergines (see page 246)
1 x 125g ball of buffalo
    mozzarella, drained
2 pinches dried oregano
freshly ground black pepper
20g vegetarian parmesan-style
    cheese, grated

To finish
20g vegetarian parmesan-style
    cheese, grated
16 basil leaves

This pizza is a riff on a classic Italian dish called melanzane alla parmigiana, made of fried aubergine slices baked with tomato sauce, mozzarella and Parmesan cheese. It's true comfort food. For our pizza version, chargrilled or roasted aubergines are piled on a base of passata, spiced up with garlic oil and chilli flakes, then topped with mozzarella and grated cheese. Sensationally good.

Melanzane

1. While your dough is rising, preheat your oven to 230°C/Fan 210°C/Gas 8. Lightly oil a couple of non-stick baking trays.

2. Dust your work surface with flour. Press and push each piece of dough into a circle about 24cm in diameter. (For more info on working with your dough, see pages 20–21.) Place your pizza bases on the baking trays.

3. Put the passata into a bowl and stir in the dessertspoon of garlic oil, the chilli flakes and chopped parsley, then stir well.

4. Using a tablespoon, spread a thin layer of the sauce over the pizza bases, taking it almost to the edges. Arrange the aubergines on top, then tear the mozzarella into small pieces and add them. Season with oregano and black pepper, then sprinkle over the grated cheese. Drizzle each pizza with a spoonful of garlic oil.

5. Place the pizzas in the preheated oven and bake for 8–10 minutes. Sprinkle with grated cheese, garnish with basil leaves and serve.

ROMANA PIZZA
For 2 Romanas you'll need 200g aubergine slices.
The other ingredients stay the same.

1 quantity of pizza dough
    (see pages 18–19)
olive oil, for greasing
75–100g spinach
flour, for dusting
120g roasted sweet potato
    purée (see page 247)
6 sweet pickled onions,
    broken into small pieces
1 small red onion, thinly sliced
130g block mozzarella, diced
2 dessertspoons garlic oil
2 pinches finely chopped
    rosemary
freshly ground black pepper

To finish
40g vegetarian parmesan-style
    cheese, grated
1 tbsp chopped parsley
2 dessertspoons chilli oil

Cipollini means 'little onions' in Italian, and these small, flattened onions have a lovely, slightly sweet flavour. They are not always easy to find, however, so it's fine to use a combination of sweet pickled onions and red onions on your pizza. With the deep orange sweet potato purée and vibrant green spinach, this pizza is a riot of colour and flavour.

Cipollini

1. While your dough is rising, preheat your oven to 230°C/Fan 210°C/Gas 8. Lightly oil a couple of non-stick baking trays.

2. Wash the spinach and trim off any tough woody stems. Put the spinach in a pan with any water clinging to the leaves and cook briefly until wilted. Tip it into a colander placed over a bowl or sink and use the back of a wooden spoon to squeeze out as much water as you can. Set aside until ready to use.

3. Dust your work surface with flour. Press and push each piece of dough into a circle about 24cm in diameter. (For more info on working with your dough, see pages 20–21.) Place your pizza bases on the baking trays.

4. Using a tablespoon, spread the sweet potato purée over the pizza bases, taking it almost to the edges. Add little dollops of spinach all over the pizzas, then add the sweet pickled onions. Divide the red onion slices evenly between the two and sprinkle over the mozzarella. Drizzle a spoonful of garlic oil over each pizza, then season with rosemary and black pepper.

5. Place the pizzas in the preheated oven and bake for 8–10 minutes. Sprinkle over the grated cheese and chopped parsley, drizzle each pizza with a spoonful of chilli oil, then serve.

ROMANA PIZZA
For 2 Romanas you'll need 160g roasted sweet potato purée, 150–200g spinach, 10 sweet pickled onions and 170g mozzarella. The other ingredients stay the same.

1 quantity of pizza dough
   (see pages 18–19)
olive oil, for greasing
120g new potatoes, scrubbed
flour, for dusting
80g béchamel sauce
   (see page 242)
1 small red onion, peeled
   and thinly sliced
1 tbsp capers
80g fontal cheese, diced
1 tbsp grated vegetarian
   parmesan-style cheese
2 pinches dried oregano
2 pinches dried or finely
   chopped fresh rosemary
freshly ground black pepper
2 dessertspoons garlic oil

To finish
1 tbsp chopped parsley
1 tbsp grated vegetarian
   parmesan-style cheese

Potato is often included in pizzas, sometimes as mash folded into the dough to produce a crust with a wonderful short texture. More often, though, thin slices of cooked potato are added on a bianca (white or béchamel sauce) base. Potato and cheese are a classic combination and this pizza is given lots of extra flavour by the addition of fontal cheese, a strong-tasting product with great melting properties that's related to the Italian fontina cheese.

Potato Fontal

1. While your dough is rising, preheat your oven to 230°C/Fan 210°C/Gas 8. Lightly oil a couple of non-stick baking trays.

2. Cook the potatoes in a pan of salted water until tender, then drain, slice thinly and set aside.

3. Dust your work surface with flour. Press and push each piece of dough into a circle about 24cm in diameter. (For more info on working with your dough, see pages 20–21.) Place your pizza bases on the baking trays.

4. Using a tablespoon, spread the béchamel over the pizza bases, taking it almost to the edges. Add the slices of onion, followed by the potatoes and capers, dividing them evenly between the pizzas. Add the diced fontal and sprinkle over the grated cheese. Season with oregano, rosemary and black pepper, then drizzle with garlic oil.

5. Place the pizzas in the preheated oven and bake for 8–10 minutes. Sprinkle over the parsley and the rest of the grated cheese, then serve.

ROMANA PIZZA
For 2 Romanas you'll need 140g béchamel, 200g potatoes, 1½ tbsp capers, 160g fontal and 40g vegetarian parmesan-style cheese – 20g for the base and 20g to finish. The other ingredients stay the same.

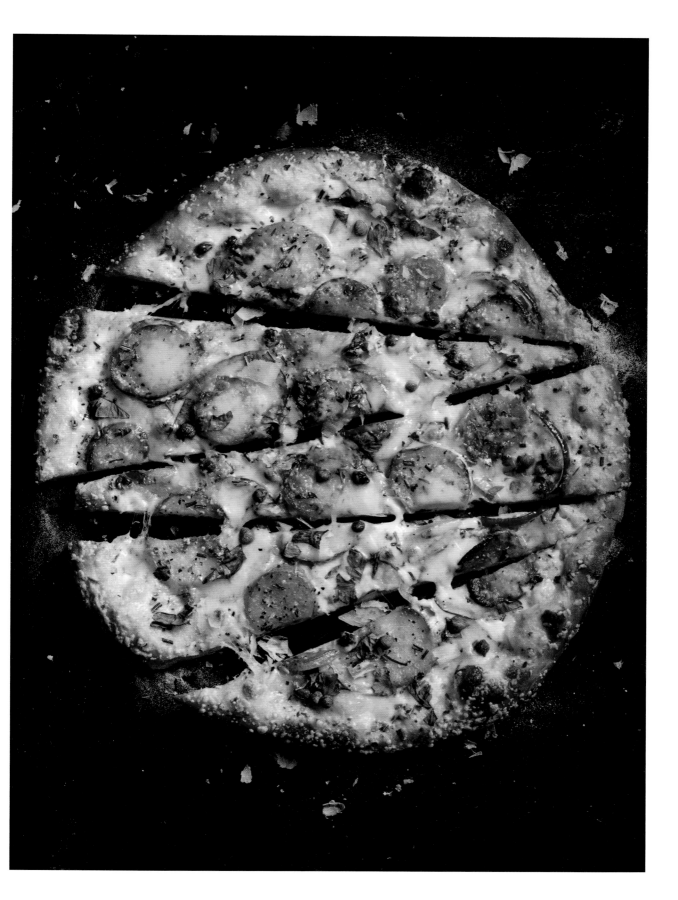

Cauliflower cheese is one of the most comforting of all dishes and here it features on a pizza! What more could anyone want? In the restaurants we like to use a very special type of onion in this recipe – Tropea onions. They are named for the beautiful Calabrian seaside town of Tropea in the region where they are grown, and are famed for their sweet flavour. Locals eat them like apples and they are held in such respect that they are known as 'la regina rossa' – the red queen. In Calabria, these small torpedo-shaped onions are eaten raw in salads, grilled or roasted, added to pizzas and frittatas – even ice cream. If you aren't lucky enough to find any, don't worry – just use slivers of regular red onion on your pizza.

Cauliflower Cheese

MAKES 2 CLASSIC PIZZAS
1 quantity of pizza dough
   (see pages 18–19)
olive oil, for greasing
flour, for dusting
100g béchamel sauce
   (see page 242)
120g cauliflower,
   cut into small pieces
1 small Tropea onion or red onion,
   peeled and cut into slivers
130g cheese (mix of pecorino,
   mozzarella, Cheddar
   or Gruyère), diced
20g vegetarian parmesan-style
   cheese, grated
2 pinches dried oregano
freshly ground black pepper
2 dessertspoons garlic oil
1 heaped tsp pine kernels

To finish
1 tbsp chopped parsley
30g vegetarian parmesan-style
   cheese shavings

1. While your dough is rising, preheat your oven to 230°C/Fan 210°C/Gas 8. Lightly oil a couple of non-stick baking trays.

2. Dust your work surface with flour. Press and push each piece of dough into a circle about 24cm in diameter. (For more info on working with your dough, see pages 20–21.) Place your pizza bases on the baking trays.

3. Using a tablespoon, spread a layer of béchamel over the pizza bases. Add the little pieces of cauliflower, followed by the onion slivers. Add the diced cheese and sprinkle over the grated cheese. Season with oregano and black pepper, then drizzle a spoonful of garlic oil over each pizza. Sprinkle a few pine kernels over the pizzas.

4. Place the pizzas in the preheated oven and bake for 8–10 minutes. Add the chopped parsley and cheese shavings, then serve.

ROMANA PIZZA
For 2 Romanas you'll need 160g béchamel, 160g cauliflower and 1 medium onion. The other ingredients stay the same.

Launched in 2001, this pizza takes its name from the Italian word '*capra*', which means goat. The key ingredient is the scrumptious, crumbled goat's cheese, topped with sweet and tangy sunblush or roasted tomatoes, making a simple but delicious flavour combination that delights all lovers of goat's cheese.

Caprina

MAKES 2 CLASSIC PIZZAS
1 quantity of pizza dough
   (see pages 18–19)
olive oil, for greasing
flour, for dusting
160g passata
2 slices (90g) goat's
   cheese, crumbled
70g block mozzarella, diced
2 pinches dried oregano
freshly ground black pepper

To finish
24 sunblush or roasted
   tomatoes from a jar

1. While your dough is rising, preheat your oven to 230°C/Fan 210°C/ Gas 8. Lightly oil a couple of non-stick baking trays.

2. Dust your work surface with flour. Press and push each piece of dough into a circle about 24cm in diameter. (For more info on working with your dough, see pages 20–21.) Place your pizza bases on the baking trays.

3. Using a tablespoon, spread a thin layer of passata over the pizza bases, taking it almost to the edges. Scatter the crumbled goat's cheese on top, then add the mozzarella, spreading both cheeses evenly over the pizzas. Season with oregano and black pepper.

4. Place the pizzas in the preheated oven and bake for 8–10 minutes. Arrange the tomatoes on top, then serve.

ROMANA PIZZA
For 2 Romanas you'll need 130g mozzarella. The other ingredients stay the same.

SPICY PIZZA

Piccante, hot, hottest, spicy or arrabbiata...call them what you will, our spicy pizzas all have one thing in common: a good hit of chilli heat. And not only does chilli add vibrant flavour that brings other ingredients alive, it also adds a great pop of colour to your pizza.

We have four main ways of adding a delicious injection of heat to pizzas.

1. With an assortment of hot peppers, some fresh (remove the seeds if you want less heat), some dried and some pickled to add a slight hint of vinegar. A combination of these works brilliantly as well.

2. By adding a few chilli flakes to the passata before using. It ensures a hit of chilli in every bite.

3. With a final drizzle of chilli flavour once your pizza is cooked. Try using chilli oil, chilli jam or a few dollops of harissa.

4. By adding meat infused with chilli. You'll see from our meat recipes that we love to add a bit of spice by slow cooking with a few chilli peppers. Sometimes the work has already been done, and 'nduja is a great example of this. Packed with fiery Calabrian chilli, this spreadable sausage is the perfect partner for pizza, as it's full of punchy flavour and almost dissolves in the heat of the oven.

Go as hot as you dare, or as your tastebuds allow. Or if you prefer a mild hum of heat, tone things down by adding a little less of the hot stuff.

MAKES 2 RECTANGULAR PIZZAS
1 quantity of pizza dough
    (see pages 18–19)
olive oil, for greasing
flour, for dusting
160g passata
90g block mozzarella, diced
2 tbsp grated Parmesan
    cheese
60g roasted peppers
    from a jar, sliced
40g fresh red chillies, diced
60g red chilli peppers
    from a jar, sliced
60g 'nduja sausage
12 slices (about 60g)
    Calabrese sausage
2 pinches dried oregano

To finish
1 x 125g ball of buffalo
    mozzarella, drained
2 tbsp grated Parmesan
    cheese
handful of rocket leaves
1 heaped tbsp pesto
    (see page 243 or
    shop-bought)

The only rectangular pizza on our menu, this recipe was inspired by ingredients from the Calabria region of southern Italy. It features Calabrese salami, a dry sausage that's made with 100 per cent pork and seasoned with hot peppers, as well as 'nduja, a spreadable sausage with a fiery chilli flavour. 'Nduja is available in supermarkets now, both on the deli counter and in jars, but if you can't find it or Calabrese sausage, use smoky, spicy Italian salami cut into slices about 1–2mm thick. With the chilli in the sausages, plus the red chillies in the topping, be prepared for this pizza to knock your socks off!

Calabrese

1. While your dough is rising, preheat your oven to 230°C/Fan 210°C/Gas 8. Lightly oil a couple of large non-stick baking trays.

2. Dust your work surface with flour. Press and push each piece of dough into a rectangle about 30 x 25cm. (For more info on working with your dough, see pages 20–21.) Place your bases on the baking trays.

3. Using a tablespoon, spread a thin layer of passata over the pizza bases, taking it almost to the edges. Divide the mozzarella between the pizzas, making sure it is evenly distributed, and then sprinkle over the grated Parmesan.

4. Add the roasted peppers and fresh chillies, then the red chilli peppers, again dividing them all between the pizzas. Add small pieces of 'nduja and the slices of Calabrese sausage, then season with oregano.

5. Place the pizzas in the preheated oven and bake for 8–10 minutes.

6. Take the cooked pizzas out of the oven and add the buffalo mozzarella, torn into pieces. Sprinkle grated Parmesan on top, then add the rocket leaves, spreading them all over the pizzas. Drizzle with the pesto, then serve.

MAKES 2 CLASSIC PIZZAS
1 quantity of pizza dough
   (see pages 18–19)
olive oil, for greasing
flour, for dusting
160g passata
6 slices (about 30g) Calabrese
   sausage or your favourite
   Italian salami
50 slices (about 100g) pepperoni
20g red chilli peppers from a jar
130g block mozzarella, diced
2 pinches dried oregano
freshly ground black pepper

To finish
6 basil leaves
30g Parmesan cheese shavings
40g (about 2½ tbsp) runny honey

At PizzaExpress, we've found that more and more customers are wanting pizzas with chilli and hot sauces – a trend that started in the USA and has taken hold in the UK. Our Hot Honey pizza was introduced to our menu in 2020 and is a very modern twist on the ever-popular American Hot.

Hot Honey

1. While your dough is rising, preheat your oven to 230°C/Fan 210°C/Gas 8. Lightly oil a couple of non-stick baking trays.

2. Dust your work surface with flour. Press and push each piece of dough into a circle about 24cm in diameter. (For more info on working with your dough, see pages 20–21.) Place your pizza bases on the baking trays.

3. Using a tablespoon, spread a thin layer of passata over the pizza bases, taking it almost to the edges. Add slices of Calabrese sausage around the edge of each pizza and then arrange the pepperoni over the pizzas, spreading the slices evenly. Scatter over the red chilli peppers and the mozzarella, then season with oregano and black pepper.

4. Place the pizzas in the preheated oven and bake for 8–10 minutes. Add the basil leaves and Parmesan shavings, then drizzle honey over the pizzas before serving.

ROMANA PIZZA
For 2 Romanas you'll need 12 slices (60g) Calabrese sausage, 60 slices (120g) pepperoni, 40g red chilli peppers, 170g mozzarella, 12 basil leaves and 60g (about 4 tbsp) runny honey. The other ingredients stay the same.

The Etna takes its name from the famous fiery volcano in Sicily and truly lives up to its reputation – this pizza is hot, hot, hot! With soft 'nduja sausage and chilli peppers ramping up the heat, you appreciate the cooling effect of the mozzarella and Parmesan cheese, as well as the salty flavour of the pancetta.

Etna

MAKES 2 CLASSIC PIZZAS
1 quantity of pizza dough
 (see pages 18–19)
olive oil, for greasing
flour, for dusting
160g passata
60g red chilli peppers
 from a jar, sliced
80g 'ndjua sausage
6 slices (60g) pancetta
130g block mozzarella, diced
20g Parmesan cheese, grated
2 pinches dried oregano
freshly ground black pepper

To finish
20g Parmesan cheese, grated

1. While your dough is rising, preheat your oven to 230°C/Fan 210°C/ Gas 8. Lightly oil a couple of non-stick baking trays.

2. Dust your work surface with flour. Press and push each piece of dough into a circle about 24cm in diameter. (For more info on working with your dough, see pages 20–21.) Place your pizza bases on the baking trays.

3. Using a tablespoon, spread a thin layer of passata over the pizza bases, taking it almost to the edges. Add the chilli peppers. Scatter small pieces of 'nduja over each base, then tear each slice of pancetta into 3 and add those too. Sprinkle over the mozzarella and the grated Parmesan and season with oregano and black pepper.

4. Place the pizzas in the preheated oven and bake for 8–10 minutes. Sprinkle with grated Parmesan and serve.

ROMANA PIZZA
For 2 Romanas you'll need 10 slices (100g) pancetta and 170g mozzarella. The other ingredients stay the same.

MAKES 2 CLASSIC PIZZAS
1 quantity of pizza dough
    (see pages 18–19)
olive oil, for greasing
flour, for dusting
160g passata
50 slices (about 100g) pepperoni
60g 'nduja sausage
40g hot green peppers
    from a jar, sliced
20g fresh red chillies,
    diced (about 2 tsp)
60g red chilli peppers
    from a jar, sliced
1 x 125g ball buffalo
    mozzarella, drained
2 pinches dried oregano
freshly ground black pepper

To finish
2 dessertspoons chilli oil
1 tbsp chopped parsley

In 2015, the fiftieth anniversary of the first PizzaExpress opening, the '65 range was introduced, elevating some iconic dishes from 1965 with extra flavoursome ingredients. This recipe turns up the heat a few notches by using a mixture of three different spicy peppers as well as fiery 'nduja sausage. Then, to cool you down, there's the creaminess of the buffalo mozzarella. Be sure to drain the mozzarella well to avoid soggy pizza.

American Hottest

1. While your dough is rising, preheat your oven to 230°C/Fan 210°C/ Gas 8. Lightly oil a couple of non-stick baking trays.

2. Dust your work surface with flour. Press and push each piece of dough into a circle about 24cm in diameter. (For more info on working with your dough, see pages 20–21.) Place your pizza bases on the baking trays.

3. Using a tablespoon, spread a thin layer of passata over the pizza bases, taking it almost to the edges. Arrange the slices of pepperoni over the pizzas, followed by small pieces of 'nduja. Add the hot green peppers, diced fresh chillies and red chilli peppers, dividing them evenly between the pizzas. Tear the mozzarella into small pieces and dot over the pizzas, then season with oregano and black pepper.

4. Place the pizzas in the preheated oven and bake for 8–10 minutes. Drizzle each pizza with a spoonful of chilli oil and sprinkle with parsley, then serve.

ROMANA PIZZA
For 2 Romanas you'll need 60 slices (120g) pepperoni and 2 balls of buffalo mozzarella. The other ingredients stay the same.

At PizzaExpress we do seem to like calling pizzas after volcanoes! This one is named for the mighty Mount Vesuvius, an active volcano near Naples in Italy. This recipe packs a chilli hit, from the pepperoni and 'nduja, and is finished with a good dash of chilli oil. The heat is balanced with a beautifully smooth sweet potato purée – a unique take on the heat and sweet trend!

Vesuvio

MAKES 2 CLASSIC PIZZAS
1 quantity of pizza dough
 (see pages 18–19)
olive oil, for greasing
flour, for dusting
120g roasted sweet potato
 purée (see page 247)
50 slices (about 100g) pepperoni
60g 'nduja sausage
130g block mozzarella, diced
2 pinches dried oregano
freshly ground black pepper

To finish
large handful of rocket leaves
30g Parmesan cheese shavings
2 dessertspoons chilli oil

1. While your dough is rising, preheat your oven to 230°C/Fan 210°C/ Gas 8. Lightly oil a couple of non-stick baking trays.

2. Dust your work surface with flour. Press and push each piece of dough into a circle about 24cm in diameter. (For more info on working with your dough, see pages 20–21.) Place your pizza bases on the baking trays.

3. Using a tablespoon, spread a layer of sweet potato purée over the pizza bases, taking it almost to the edges. Arrange the slices of pepperoni evenly over the pizzas, then add small pieces of 'nduja, placing them in between the pepperoni. Sprinkle the mozzarella over, then season with oregano and black pepper.

4. Place the pizzas in the preheated oven and bake for 8–10 minutes. Add the rocket leaves and Parmesan shavings, then drizzle a spoonful of chilli oil all over each pizza before serving.

ROMANA PIZZA
For 2 Romanas you'll need 160g sweet potato purée, 80g 'nduja and 170g mozzarella. The other ingredients stay the same.

Calzone is a pizza with a difference – the toppings are on the inside. Stuffed with a generous helping of filling and with a crispy top, this is a hearty feast of a pizza. Just make sure you seal it well. A spicy, spreadable sausage from Calabria, southern Italy, 'nduja has become hugely popular in the UK in recent years. 'Nduja lovers spread it on toast, mix it into sauces, dollop it onto pasta and, of course, add it to pizzas!

Calzone 'Nduja

MAKES 2 CALZONES
1 quantity of pizza dough
    (see pages 18–19)
olive oil, for greasing
flour, for dusting
160g passata
50 slices (about 100g) pepperoni
60g 'nduja sausage
40g red chilli peppers
    from a jar, sliced
40g hot green peppers
    from a jar, sliced
20g fresh red chilli, diced
80g block mozzarella, diced
2 pinches dried oregano
freshly ground black pepper

Topping
olive oil, for brushing
4 slices (40g) pancetta, halved
20g Parmesan cheese, grated

1. While your dough is rising, preheat your oven to 230°C/Fan 210°C/Gas 8. Lightly oil a couple of non-stick baking trays.

2. Dust your work surface with flour. Press and push each piece of dough into a circle about 26cm in diameter – slightly larger than the usual base. (For more info on working with your dough, see pages 20–21.) Place your pizza bases on the baking trays.

3. Using a tablespoon, spread a layer of passata over half of each pizza base, leaving about 3cm around the edge. Add the slices of pepperoni over the passata, then the 'nduja, torn into pieces. Add the chilli peppers and fresh chilli, followed by the mozzarella, dividing each ingredient equally between the pizza halves. Season with oregano and black pepper.

4. Using a pastry brush, brush a little chilled water around the edge of each base. Then fold the empty half of the calzone over the filling so the edges meet. Press along the edge of each calzone to seal together and crimp with your fingers. If you have a pastry crimper, run that around the edge and pull away any excess dough.

5. Brush the pizzas with oil, top each calzone with 4 slices of pancetta and sprinkle with grated Parmesan. Place in the preheated oven and bake for 8–10 minutes.

MAKES 2 CLASSIC PIZZAS
1 quantity of pizza dough
    (see pages 18–19)
olive oil, for greasing
flour, for dusting
160g passata
12 slices (about 60g) chorizo
60g roasted red peppers
    from a jar, sliced
60g sweet red peppers
    from a jar, torn into pieces
70g block mozzarella, diced
70g goat's cheese
2 pinches dried oregano
freshly ground black pepper
2 dessertspoons garlic oil

To finish
handful of rocket leaves
20g Parmesan cheese shavings

For this pizza, we move away from Italian flavours and use chorizo, a cured, smoked sausage from Spain. The spicy taste of the sausage is balanced with creamy goat's cheese and mozzarella, as well as juicy red peppers. The word '*amore*' means 'love' in Italian and we know you're going to love this recipe.

Amore

1. While your dough is rising, preheat your oven to 230°C/Fan 210°C/ Gas 8. Lightly oil a couple of non-stick baking trays.

2. Dust your work surface with flour. Press and push each piece of dough into a circle about 24cm in diameter. (For more info on working with your dough, see pages 20–21.) Place your pizza bases on the baking trays.

3. Using a tablespoon, spread a thin layer of passata over the pizza bases, taking it almost to the edges. Add the slices of chorizo, arranging them all over the bases. Then add the roasted peppers and the pieces of torn sweet red peppers, dividing them equally between the pizzas. Sprinkle with the mozzarella and crumble over the goat's cheese. Season with oregano and black pepper, then drizzle each pizza with a spoonful of garlic oil.

4. Place the pizzas in the preheated oven and bake for 8–10 minutes. Top each pizza with rocket leaves and Parmesan shavings, then serve.

ROMANA PIZZA
For 2 Romanas you'll need 24 slices (120g) chorizo and 90g mozzarella. The other ingredients stay the same.

You'll find our fabulous spicy pulled lamb recipe on page 249. Yes, it does have to cook for hours, but it's very little work to put together and once the lamb is in the oven you can leave it be and just enjoy the wonderful aromas. If you can't wait and you have some leftover roast lamb, this is the perfect way to use it up. Cut the meat into small pieces, removing any fatty bits, and sprinkle your pizza with some cumin and coriander seeds to add flavour.

MAKES 2 CLASSIC PIZZAS
1 quantity of pizza dough
   (see pages 18–19)
olive oil, for greasing
flour, for dusting
160g passata
1 small red onion,
   peeled and thinly sliced
100g pulled spiced lamb
   (see page 249)
130g block mozzarella, diced
2 pinches dried oregano
freshly ground black pepper

To finish
20g pomegranate seeds
2 tsp chopped mint
2 dessertspoons chilli oil

Pulled Lamb

1. While your dough is rising, preheat your oven to 230°C/Fan 210°C/Gas 8. Lightly oil a couple of non-stick baking trays.

2. Dust your work surface with flour. Press and push each piece of dough into a circle about 24cm in diameter. (For more info on working with your dough, see pages 20–21.) Place your pizza bases on the baking trays.

3. Using a tablespoon, spread a thin layer of passata over the pizza bases, taking it almost to the edges. Add the slices of red onion, then small spoonfuls of the pulled lamb, arranging it evenly over the pizzas. Add the mozzarella and season with oregano and black pepper.

4. Place the pizzas in the preheated oven and bake for 8–10 minutes. Sprinkle over the pomegranate seeds and chopped mint, then drizzle each pizza with a spoonful of chilli oil.

ROMANA PIZZA
For 2 Romanas you'll need 140g pulled lamb, 170g mozzarella and 30g pomegranate seeds. The other ingredients stay the same.

This pizza certainly zaps you with flavour. It's laden with chicken, 'nduja sausage and cheese, all on a beautiful base of creamed corn, and given a touch of heat with chilli oil and red chilli pepper pearls. Scrumptious.

Zapparoli

MAKES 2 CLASSIC PIZZAS
1 quantity of pizza dough
(see pages 18–19)
olive oil, for greasing
flour, for dusting
120g creamed corn
from a tin
140g cooked chicken,
torn into small pieces
60g 'nduja sausage
130g block mozzarella, diced
2 tsp grated Parmesan cheese
2 pinches dried oregano
freshly ground black pepper
2 dessertspoons garlic oil

To finish
20 red chilli pepper pearls
chopped parsley

1. While your dough is rising, preheat your oven to 230°C/Fan 210°C/Gas 8. Lightly oil a couple of non-stick baking trays.

2. Dust your work surface with flour. Press and push each piece of dough into a circle about 24cm in diameter. (For more info on working with your dough, see pages 20–21.) Place your pizza bases on the baking trays.

3. Using a tablespoon, spread the creamed corn over the pizza bases, taking it almost to the edges. Add the pieces of chicken, then small pieces of 'nduja, dividing both equally between the pizzas. Add the mozzarella and sprinkle over the grated Parmesan. Season with oregano and black pepper, then drizzle a spoonful of garlic oil over each pizza.

4. Place the pizzas in the preheated oven and bake for 8–10 minutes. Add the chilli pepper pearls and finish with chopped parsley.

ROMANA PIZZA
For 2 Romanas you'll need 200g creamed corn, 170g mozzarella and 28 red chilli pepper pearls. The other ingredients stay the same.

The Barbacoa has a legion of devoted fans. We've added the recipe for the pulled barbacoa beef on page 248 so you can make a fully authentic version at home. The recipe makes more than you need for a couple of pizzas, but the trick is to freeze the rest in portions so you can whip together your favourite in no time on another occasion. Or if you're short of time and have some leftover roast beef, just chop it into small pieces and coat it in chipotle salsa for a super-quick and tasty version of the original.

Barbacoa

MAKES 2 CLASSIC PIZZAS
1 quantity of pizza dough
    (see pages 18–19)
olive oil, for greasing
flour, for dusting
160g passata
60g chipotle salsa
    from a jar
160g barbacoa beef
    (see page 248)
130g block mozzarella, diced
2 pinches dried oregano
freshly ground black pepper
2 dessertspoons garlic oil

Bruschetta mix
1 vine tomato, diced
¼ red onion, peeled
    and diced

To finish
chopped coriander

1. While your dough is rising, preheat your oven to 230°C/Fan 210°C/ Gas 8. Lightly oil a couple of non-stick baking trays.

2. Combine the tomato and red onion for the bruschetta mix in a bowl and season with black pepper.

3. Dust your work surface with flour. Press and push each piece of dough into a circle about 24cm in diameter. (For more info on working with your dough, see pages 20–21.) Place your pizza bases on the baking trays.

4. Using a tablespoon, spread a thin layer of passata over the pizza bases, taking it almost to the edges. Drizzle dollops of chipotle salsa evenly over the pizzas, then tear the beef into small chunks and add them too. Sprinkle over the mozzarella and season with oregano and black pepper. Drizzle a spoonful of garlic oil over each pizza.

5. Place the pizzas in the preheated oven and bake for 8–10 minutes. Top with the bruschetta mix, spreading it evenly over the pizzas, and finish with chopped coriander.

ROMANA PIZZA
For 2 Romanas you'll need 80g chipotle salsa, 200g barbacoa beef, 170g mozzarella and double the amount of bruschetta mix. The other ingredients stay the same.

SEAFOOD PIZZA

Peter was a pescatarian, which meant that he ate fish but no meat. So this is why in so many of our Heritage recipes you'll find one of his favourite ingredients: anchovies. These tasty little fish feature on some of our seafood pizzas as well. When we looked back through the seafood recipes in our archive, we found some interesting examples. For instance, there was one called Pizza San Terenzio, which was topped with oysters, and another named Connoisseur, which was made with red and black caviar and styled like a roulette wheel! Clearly for those special customers who liked to play a little pizza roulette as they ate.

For this chapter, though, we have selected our traditional favourites, which we know you'll enjoy making and, most importantly, eating.

MAKES 2 CLASSIC PIZZAS
1 quantity of pizza dough
    (see pages 18–19)
olive oil, for greasing
flour, for dusting
20g garlic cloves,
    peeled and crushed
100g béchamel sauce
    (see page 242)
12 cooked king prawns,
    shelled and deveined
60g roasted peppers
    from a jar, sliced
130g block mozzarella, diced
freshly ground black pepper

Bruschetta mix
1 vine tomato, diced
½ small red onion,
    peeled and diced

To finish
chopped parsley

In Italy, this pizza is known as a '*gamberi*' – the Italian word for prawns. It is a very classy-looking pizza with a white base of creamy béchamel sauce topped with roasted peppers and mozzarella as well as beautiful juicy prawns.

Garlic Prawn

1. While your dough is rising, preheat your oven to 230°C/Fan 210°C/Gas 8. Lightly oil a couple of non-stick baking trays.

2. For the bruschetta mix, combine the tomato and onion in a bowl and season with pepper. Set aside.

3. Dust your work surface with flour. Press and push each piece of dough into a circle about 24cm in diameter. (For more info on working with your dough, see pages 20–21.) Place your pizza bases on the baking trays.

4. Stir the crushed garlic into the béchamel sauce. Using a tablespoon, spread a thin layer of béchamel over the pizza bases, taking it almost to the edges. Add the prawns and peppers, then sprinkle over the mozzarella. Season with black pepper.

5. Place the pizzas in the preheated oven and bake for 8–10 minutes. Add the bruschetta mix, dividing it between the pizzas, and finish with chopped parsley.

ROMANA PIZZA
For 2 Romanas you'll need 160g béchamel sauce, 170g mozzarella and 16 king prawns. The other ingredients stay the same.

MAKES 2 CLASSIC PIZZAS
1 quantity of pizza dough
    (see pages 18–19)
olive oil, for greasing
flour, for dusting
160g passata
1 small red onion,
    peeled and thinly sliced
12 black olives, pitted
6 cherry tomatoes, halved
120g tinned tuna, drained
70g block mozzarella, diced
2 tbsp (60g) mascarpone
    mixed with 200g passata
2 pinches oregano
freshly ground black pepper
2 tsp olive oil

To finish
1 tbsp chopped parsley

Tinned tuna is such a useful ingredient – and everyone has some in the store cupboard. Here, delicious chunks of tuna are combined with olives, cherry tomatoes and mozzarella, then topped with generous spoonfuls of a creamy mix of mascarpone and tomato. A feast of flavour.

Al Tonno

1. While your dough is rising, preheat your oven to 230°C/Fan 210°C/Gas 8. Lightly oil a couple of non-stick baking trays.

2. Dust your work surface with flour. Press and push each piece of dough into a circle about 24cm in diameter. (For more info on working with your dough, see pages 20–21.) Place your pizza bases on the baking trays.

3. Using a tablespoon, spread a thin layer of passata over the pizza bases, taking it almost to the edges. Scatter the onion slices, olives and tomatoes over the pizzas, dividing them evenly, then add little chunks of tuna. Add the mozzarella, then dot 4 tablespoons of the mascarpone and passata mix over each pizza. Season with oregano and black pepper and drizzle each pizza with a teaspoon of olive oil.

4. Place the pizzas in the preheated oven and bake for 8–10 minutes. Finish with chopped parsley and serve.

ROMANA PIZZA
For 2 Romanas you'll need 16 black olives, 8 cherry tomatoes, 140g tuna and 100g mozzarella. The other ingredients stay the same.

First listed on our menu in 1993, this pizza is named after the region of Italy it comes from – Sicily, of course! It includes ingredients typical of Sicilian cooking, such as artichokes, olives and anchovies, which combine to make a harmonious balance of flavours and a super-tasty pizza.

Siciliana

MAKES 2 CLASSIC PIZZAS
1 quantity of pizza dough
    (see pages 18–19)
olive oil, for greasing
flour, for dusting
160g passata
12 black olives, pitted
8 chargrilled artichoke quarters
    from a jar (about 100g),
    torn into pieces
2 slices (60g) ham
6 brown anchovies from
    a jar or tin
130g block mozzarella, diced
2 pinches oregano
freshly ground black pepper
2 dessertspoons garlic oil

1. While your dough is rising, preheat your oven to 230°C/Fan 210°C/Gas 8. Lightly oil a couple of non-stick baking trays.

2. Dust your work surface with flour. Press and push each piece of dough into a circle about 24cm in diameter. (For more info on working with your dough, see pages 20–21.) Place your pizza bases on the baking trays.

3. Using a tablespoon, spread a thin layer of passata over the pizza bases, taking it almost to the edges. Arrange 6 olives around the edge of each pizza. Divide the artichokes equally over the pizza bases, then tear each slice of ham into about 7 pieces and add to the pizzas.

4. Place 3 anchovies on each pizza, arranging them from the edge towards the centre like clock hands. Add the mozzarella and season with oregano and black pepper. Drizzle each pizza with a spoonful of garlic oil.

5. Place the pizzas in the preheated oven and bake for 8–10 minutes.

ROMANA PIZZA
For 2 Romanas you'll need 16 black olives and 170g mozzarella. The other ingredients stay the same.

The Neptune pizza appeared on our very first menu, back in 1965, and features a robust mix of toppings traditionally used in pizzas all over Italy. Tuna, capers and olives are a classic combination and work perfectly together. There's no cheese in this recipe – so ideal for pizza-lovers on a dairy-free diet – so we use more passata than normal to keep it nice and juicy.

Neptune

MAKES 2 CLASSIC PIZZAS
1 quantity of pizza dough
    (see pages 18–19)
olive oil, for greasing
flour, for dusting
240g passata
12 black olives, pitted
1 small red onion,
    peeled and thinly sliced
1 tbsp capers
140g tinned tuna, drained
6 brown anchovies from
    a jar or tin
2 pinches dried oregano
freshly ground black pepper

To finish
1 tbsp chopped parsley
2 lemon wedges

1. While your dough is rising, preheat your oven to 230°C/Fan 210°C/ Gas 8. Lightly oil a couple of non-stick baking trays.

2. Dust your work surface with flour. Press and push each piece of dough into a circle about 24cm in diameter. (For more info on working with your dough, see pages 20–21.) Place your pizza bases on the baking trays.

3. Using a tablespoon, spread a layer of passata over the pizza bases and arrange 6 olives around the edge of each base. Add the slices of onion and the capers, then flake the tuna and divide it evenly between the pizzas. Arrange 3 anchovies on each pizza, placing them from the edge towards the centre like clock hands. Season with oregano and black pepper.

4. Place the pizzas in the preheated oven and bake for 8–10 minutes. Sprinkle over the parsley and serve garnished with lemon wedges.

ROMANA PIZZA
For 2 Romanas you'll need 16 black olives and 1½ tbsp capers. The other ingredients stay the same.

1 quantity of pizza dough
  (see pages 18–19)
olive oil, for greasing
2 free-range eggs,
  room temperature
flour, for dusting
160g passata
12 black olives, pitted
2 slices (60g) ham
1 tbsp capers
60g roasted peppers
  from a jar, sliced
6 brown anchovies
  from a jar or tin
130g block mozzarella, diced
2 pinches dried oregano
freshly ground black pepper
2 tsp olive oil

The word 'capricciosa' means 'capricious' or 'unpredictable'. People say this pizza got its name because when it was first invented in Italy, chefs would add whatever ingredients were left over at the end of the day, so you were never quite sure what you were getting!

Capricciosa

1. While your dough is rising, preheat your oven to 230°C/Fan 210°C/ Gas 8. Lightly oil a couple of non-stick baking trays.

2. To hard-boil your eggs, first make sure they are at room temperature. Put the eggs in a pan, cover with cold water and bring to the boil. Simmer for 7 or 8 minutes, then remove and place under cold running water until cool. Peel and set aside.

3. Dust your work surface with flour. Press and push each piece of dough into a circle about 24cm in diameter. (For more info on working with your dough, see pages 20–21.) Place your pizza bases on the baking trays.

4. Using a tablespoon, spread a thin layer of passata over the pizza bases, taking it almost to the edges. Arrange 6 black olives around the edge of each pizza. Slice each hard-boiled egg into 6 and place these between the olives. Tear each slice of ham into about 7 pieces and add these to the pizzas, then add the capers and roasted peppers, dividing them all evenly.

5. Arrange 3 anchovies on each pizza, placing them from the edge towards the centre like clock hands. Add the mozzarella and season the pizzas with oregano and black pepper. Drizzle each pizza with a teaspoon of olive oil.

6. Place the pizzas in the preheated oven and bake for 8–10 minutes.

ROMANA PIZZA
For 2 Romanas you'll need 16 black olives, 1½ tbsp capers and 170g mozzarella. The other ingredients stay the same.

This pizza has a special place in our Heritage range, as it was Peter's favourite and has been on the menu since day one. At his local PizzaExpress in Peterborough, Peter had his very own till button for his food, which included his beloved Napoletana. It's simple, classic and delicious – definitely one for anchovy lovers.

Napoletana

MAKES 2 CLASSIC PIZZAS
1 quantity of pizza dough
   (see pages 18–19)
olive oil, for greasing
flour, for dusting
160g passata
12 black olives, pitted
1 tbsp capers
6 brown anchovies
   from a jar or tin
130g block mozzarella, diced
2 pinches dried oregano
freshly ground black pepper
2 dessertspoons garlic oil

1. While your dough is rising, preheat your oven to 230°C/Fan 210°C/Gas 8. Lightly oil a couple of non-stick baking trays.

2. Dust your work surface with flour. Press and push each piece of dough into a circle about 24cm in diameter. (For more info on working with your dough, see pages 20–21.) Place your pizza bases on the baking trays.

3. Using a tablespoon, spread a thin layer of passata over the pizza bases, taking it almost to the edges. Arrange 6 black olives around the edge of each pizza, then scatter over the capers. Add 3 anchovies to each pizza, placing them from the edge towards the centre, like clock hands. Add the mozzarella, then season with oregano and black pepper. Drizzle a spoonful of garlic oil over each pizza.

4. Place the pizzas in the preheated oven and bake for 8–10 minutes.

ROMANA PIZZA
For 2 Romanas you'll need 16 black olives, 1½ tbsp capers, 10 brown anchovies and 170g mozzarella. The other ingredients stay the same.

Nice, in the south of France, is a city famed for its culinary wonders and the term 'Niçoise' is applied to many dishes, one of the most famous being salade Niçoise. The traditional ingredients of the salad – tuna, olives, anchovy, tomato, egg – also happen to work brilliantly on a pizza, so both options are on our menu.

Niçoise

MAKES 2 CLASSIC PIZZAS
1 quantity of pizza dough
(see pages 18–19)
olive oil, for greasing
2 free-range eggs,
room temperature
flour, for dusting
160g passata
12 black olives, pitted
80g tinned tuna, drained
6 brown anchovies
from a jar or tin
1 tbsp capers
6 baby plum tomatoes, halved
130g block mozzarella, diced
2 pinches dried oregano
freshly ground black pepper
2 dessertspoons garlic oil

To finish
handful of rocket leaves
chopped parsley
2 dessertspoons extra
virgin olive oil
lemon wedges

1. While your dough is rising, preheat your oven to 230°C/Fan 210°C/Gas 8. Lightly oil a couple of non-stick baking trays.

2. To hard-boil your eggs, first make sure they are at room temperature. Put the eggs in a pan, cover with cold water and bring to the boil. Simmer for 7 or 8 minutes, then remove and place under cold running water until cool. Peel and set aside.

3. Dust your work surface with flour. Press and push each piece of dough into a circle about 24cm in diameter. (For more info on working with your dough, see pages 20–21.) Place your pizza bases on the baking trays.

4. Using a tablespoon, spread a thin layer of passata over the pizza bases, taking it almost to the edges. Arrange 6 olives around the edge of each pizza. Slice each hard-boiled egg into 6 and place the slices between the olives. Flake the tuna over the pizzas, dividing it evenly, then add 3 anchovies to each pizza, placing them from the edge towards the centre like clock hands. Add the capers and tomato halves, sprinkle over the mozzarella and season with oregano and black pepper. Drizzle a spoonful of garlic oil over each pizza.

5. Place the pizzas in the preheated oven and bake for 8–10 minutes. Add the rocket leaves and parsley, drizzle over the extra virgin olive oil, then serve with lemon wedges.

ROMANA PIZZA
For 2 Romanas you'll need 16 black olives, 140g tuna, 1 heaped tbsp capers and 170g mozzarella. The other ingredients stay the same.

MEAT
PIZZA

Our opening menu in 1965 featured ten pizzas, and only one of them contained meat: the American, named in honour of a girlfriend of Peter's. It was topped with mozzarella, passata and pepperoni sausage and is still on our menu today.

Since those days we have developed many more meat recipes, but pork remains the mainstay of our selection. From slow-cooked pulled pork to thinly sliced cured ham, pepperoni and slices of sausage and pancetta, pork just works on pizza and adds an abundance of flavour. But we have also worked to develop recipes using other types of meat, and now chicken, lamb and beef recipes have all earned their place on the menu.

It's all too easy to get caught up in the idea that a meat pizza must have lots of meat on it – but this isn't the case. When it comes to pizza, meat is more about flavour than bulk. Adding a few slices of pancetta acts as a great seasoning to make a pizza super tasty (we never add extra salt to our pizzas) and helps to showcase the other ingredients, which may be veg or another meat. But, of course, there are times when meat is truly the star – porchetta anyone?

Most meats are already cooked or cured before they go on to a pizza, so with the fierce heat of the pizza oven there's a danger the topping could dry out. We use a lot of pulled meats – which have been slow cooked for many hours – on our pizzas for two reasons. First, the long, slow cook keeps the meat beautifully moist and succulent. And second, this way of cooking imparts loads of flavour, whether spicy, herby or smoky.

Using the best ingredients is key to ensuring a great-tasting pizza. As you don't need a huge amount of meat because you don't want to overload your pizza, choose the best you can afford. Supermarkets often have a good range of cured meats, but if you have a good Italian deli near where you live – even better!

First launched in the early 2000s, the Parmense is a celebration of some of the Parma region's greatest produce: Parma ham and Parmesan cheese. The salty, meaty flavour of the ham is balanced by the rich egg and crisp asparagus to make a perfect marriage of ingredients. Supermarkets stock asparagus all year round now, and your pizza will taste great whenever you make it, but try to take advantage of British asparagus, in the shops from late April to June.

Parmense

MAKES 2 CLASSIC PIZZAS
1 quantity of pizza dough
    (see pages 18–19)
olive oil, for greasing
flour, for dusting
160g passata
8 asparagus spears
130g block mozzarella, diced
2 pinches dried oregano
freshly ground black pepper
2 tsp olive oil
2 free-range eggs

To finish
4 slices (60g) Parma ham
30g Parmesan cheese, grated

1. While your dough is rising, preheat your oven to 230°C/Fan 210°C/ Gas 8. Lightly oil a couple of non-stick baking trays.

2. Dust your work surface with flour. Press and push each piece of dough into a circle about 24cm in diameter. (For more info on working with your dough, see pages 20–21.) Place your pizza bases on the baking trays.

3. Using a tablespoon, spread a thin layer of passata over the pizza bases, taking it almost to the edges. Add 4 asparagus spears to each pizza, arranging them in a box shape and leaving space in the middle for the egg. Add the mozzarella, leaving the centre clear. Season with oregano and black pepper and drizzle a teaspoon of oil over each pizza.

4. If you prefer your eggs cooked through, crack an egg into the centre of each pizza, place them in the preheated oven and bake for 8–10 minutes. If you prefer soft eggs, cook the pizzas for 4–5 minutes first, then add the eggs and cook for another 4–5 minutes.

5. Add 2 slices of Parma ham to each pizza, placing them either side of the egg, scatter over the grated Parmesan, then serve.

ROMANA PIZZA
For 2 Romanas you'll need 12 asparagus spears and 170g mozzarella. The other ingredients stay the same.

Spaghetti alla carbonara is one of the most popular of all pasta dishes, and here it is reimagined as a pizza topping. The ultimate in comfort food, our pizza version has a wonderful balance of creamy béchamel and salty, crisp pancetta, topped with a soft egg to add that extra touch of luxury. As a finishing touch, this pizza really benefits from a generous grinding of pepper to cut through the richness.

Carbonara

MAKES 2 CLASSIC PIZZAS
1 quantity of pizza dough
    (see pages 18–19)
olive oil, for greasing
flour, for dusting
100g béchamel sauce
    (see page 242)
8 slices (80g) pancetta
    (or streaky bacon rashers)
130g block mozzarella, diced
20g Parmesan cheese, grated
freshly ground black pepper
2 dessertspoons garlic oil
2 free-range eggs

To finish
20g Parmesan cheese, grated
chopped parsley

1. While your dough is rising, preheat your oven to 230°C/Fan 210°C/Gas 8. Lightly oil a couple of non-stick baking trays.

2. Dust your work surface with flour. Press and push each piece of dough into a circle about 24cm in diameter. (For more info on working with your dough, see pages 20–21.) Place your pizza bases on the baking trays.

3. Using a tablespoon, spread a thin layer of béchamel over the pizza bases, taking it almost to the edges. Arrange the pancetta on the bases, leaving a space in the middle of each for the egg. Add the mozzarella and sprinkle over the grated Parmesan, again leaving the centres clear. Season with black pepper, then drizzle a spoonful of garlic oil over each pizza.

4. If you prefer your eggs cooked through, crack an egg into the centre of each pizza, place them in the preheated oven and bake for 8–10 minutes. If you prefer soft eggs, cook the pizzas for 4–5 minutes first, then add the eggs and cook for another 4–5 minutes.

5. Sprinkle over the grated cheese and garnish with parsley, then serve.

ROMANA PIZZA
For 2 Romanas you'll need 160g béchamel, 12 slices (120g) pancetta or bacon and 170g mozzarella. The other ingredients stay the same.

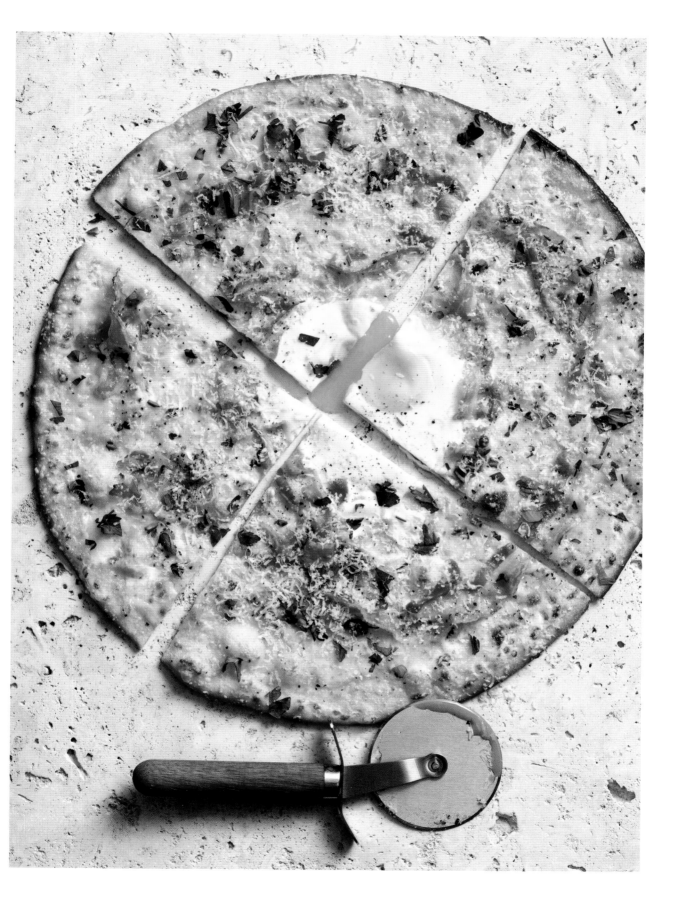

1 quantity of pizza dough
  (see pages 18–19)
olive oil, for greasing
flour, for dusting
160g passata
2 roasted peppers from
  a jar, sliced
60g cooked chicken
4 slices (40g) pancetta
130g block mozzarella, diced
freshly ground black pepper

To finish
chopped parsley

The name gives this one away – a classic combination of chicken and pancetta makes this a tasty dish to satisfy the most ardent carnivore. The extra level of flavour from the sweet roasted peppers works brilliantly with the meats and mozzarella.

Pollo Pancetta

1. While your dough is rising, preheat your oven to 230°C/Fan 210°C/Gas 8. Lightly oil a couple of non-stick baking trays.

2. Dust your work surface with flour. Press and push each piece of dough into a circle about 24cm in diameter. (For more info on working with your dough, see pages 20–21.) Place your pizza bases on the baking trays.

3. Using a tablespoon, spread a thin layer of passata over the pizza bases, taking it almost to the edges. Add the slices of roasted pepper, then tear the chicken into pieces and divide them evenly between the pizzas. Arrange the slices of pancetta between the chicken and scatter over the mozzarella. Season with black pepper.

4. Place the pizzas in the preheated oven and bake for 8–10 minutes. Garnish with chopped parsley, then serve.

ROMANA PIZZA
For 2 Romanas you'll need 3 roasted peppers, 80g cooked chicken, 6 slices (60g) pancetta and 170g mozzarella. The other ingredients stay the same.

Almost anything finished with a generous helping of pesto is delicious and this pizza is no exception. The simple flavours of chicken and spinach sit on a layer of creamy béchamel instead of passata, and the whole is enhanced with the punchy, herbal hit of pesto and sunblush tomatoes. This embodies all our pizza know-how – simple, good ingredients and big flavours. It's a winner.

Pollo Italiano

MAKES 2 CLASSIC PIZZAS
1 quantity of pizza dough
   (see pages 18–19)
olive oil, for greasing
75–100g spinach
flour, for dusting
100g béchamel sauce
   (see page 242)
160g cooked chicken
130g block mozzarella, diced
2 dessertspoons garlic oil
freshly ground black pepper

To finish
40g (2 heaped tbsp) pesto
   (see page 243 or shop-bought)
16 sunblush tomatoes

1. While your dough is rising, preheat your oven to 230°C/Fan 210°C/Gas 8. Lightly oil a couple of non-stick baking trays.

2. Wash the spinach and trim off any tough woody stems. Put the spinach in a pan with any water clinging to the leaves and cook briefly until wilted. Tip it into a colander placed over a bowl or sink and use the back of a wooden spoon to squeeze out as much water as you can. Set aside until ready to use.

3. Dust your work surface with flour. Press and push each piece of dough into a circle about 24cm in diameter. (For more info on working with your dough, see pages 20–21.) Place your pizza bases on the baking trays.

4. Using a tablespoon, spread a thin layer of béchamel over the pizza bases. Tear the chicken into pieces and add to the pizzas, dividing it evenly between them, followed by dollops of spinach. Add the mozzarella and drizzle a spoonful of garlic oil over each pizza. Season with black pepper.

5. Place in the preheated oven and bake for 8–10 minutes. Drizzle with the pesto and finish with the sunblush tomatoes, then serve.

ROMANA PIZZA
For 2 Romanas you'll need 160g béchamel sauce, 200g cooked chicken and 170g mozzarella. The other ingredients stay the same.

With one of our more unusual pizza names, the Pinglestone is a celebration of watercress. It's named for the watercress beds of Pinglestone in Alresford, Hampshire, which has been labelled 'the watercress capital of the UK'. Famed for its peppery bite, watercress is part of the mustard family and adds a great fresh flavour and texture to this pizza. It's available all year round but at its best from April to September. You can use rocket leaves instead for that peppery taste, but do give watercress a try if you can.

Pinglestone

MAKES 2 CLASSIC PIZZAS
1 quantity of pizza dough
   (see pages 18–19)
olive oil, for greasing
flour, for dusting
160g passata
8 slices (80g) pancetta
130g block mozzarella, diced
freshly ground black pepper
2 free-range eggs

To finish
handful of watercress
30g Parmesan cheese shavings
2 dessertspoons extra virgin
   olive oil

1. While your dough is rising, preheat your oven to 230°C/Fan 210°C/Gas 8. Lightly oil a couple of non-stick baking trays.

2. Dust your work surface with flour. Press and push each piece of dough into a circle about 24cm in diameter. (For more info on working with your dough, see pages 20–21.) Place your pizza bases on the baking trays.

3. Using a tablespoon, spread a thin layer of passata over the pizza bases, taking it almost to the edges. Arrange the pancetta and mozzarella evenly over the pizzas, leaving a space in the centre of each for the eggs, and season with black pepper.

4. If you prefer your eggs cooked through, crack an egg into the centre of each pizza, place them in the preheated oven and bake for 8–10 minutes. If you prefer soft eggs, cook the pizzas for 4–5 minutes first, then add the eggs and cook for another 4–5 minutes.

5. Add the watercress and sprinkle over the Parmesan shavings, then drizzle a spoonful of oil over each pizza and serve.

ROMANA PIZZA
For 2 Romanas you'll need 10 slices (100g) pancetta, 170g mozzarella and 40g Parmesan cheese shavings. The other ingredients stay the same.

This very special pizza is inspired by the popular Chinese dish, crispy duck with pancakes. You can use leftover roast duck, or for a really quick and easy pizza feast, buy a beautiful roast duck from your local Chinese takeaway.

Anatra

MAKES 2 CLASSIC PIZZAS
1 quantity of pizza dough
   (see pages 18–19)
olive oil, for greasing
flour, for dusting
80g hoisin sauce
   from a jar
1 small red onion,
   peeled and thinly sliced
100g courgette, grated
120g roast duck
130g block mozzarella, diced
freshly ground black pepper

To finish
handful of rocket leaves
60g spring onions, chopped

1. While your dough is rising, preheat your oven to 230°C/Fan 210°C/ Gas 8. Lightly oil a couple of non-stick baking trays.

2. Dust your work surface with flour. Press and push each piece of dough into a circle about 24cm in diameter. (For more info on working with your dough, see pages 20–21.) Place your pizza bases on the baking trays.

3. Using a tablespoon, spread a thin layer of hoisin sauce over the pizza bases, taking it almost to the edges. Add the slices of red onion, then the grated courgette. Pull the duck meat into shreds and spread it over the pizzas, then add the mozzarella. Season with black pepper.

4. Place the pizzas in the preheated oven and bake for 8–10 minutes. Sprinkle over the rocket leaves and spring onions and serve.

ROMANA PIZZA
For 2 Romanas you'll need 120g hoisin sauce, 140g courgette, 200g roast duck and 170g mozzarella. The other ingredients stay the same.

Anyone who has worked for PizzaExpress since 2005 will be very familiar with this pizza. The combination of béchamel, mushroom and chicken, with a little bite of onion, is perfect refuelling food and it's an absolute team favourite. It was off the menu for over ten years but was asked for so often that we brought it back as a delivery exclusive in 2020, much to the delight of our customers and teams.

Pollo con Funghi

MAKES 2 CLASSIC PIZZAS
1 quantity of pizza dough
    (see pages 18–19)
olive oil, for greasing
flour, for dusting
100g béchamel sauce
    (see page 242)
1 small red onion,
    peeled and thinly sliced
80g cup mushrooms,
    wiped and sliced
140g cooked chicken
130g block mozzarella, diced
freshly ground black pepper

To finish
chopped parsley

1. While your dough is rising, preheat your oven to 230°C/Fan 210°C/Gas 8. Lightly oil a couple of non-stick baking trays.

2. Dust your work surface with flour. Press and push each piece of dough into a circle about 24cm in diameter. (For more info on working with your dough, see pages 20–21.) Place your pizza bases on the baking trays.

3. Using a tablespoon, spread a thin layer of béchamel over the pizza bases, taking it almost to the edges. Add the slices of onion and mushroom, spreading them evenly over the bases. Tear the chicken into pieces and divide between the pizzas, then scatter over the mozzarella. Season with black pepper.

4. Place the pizzas in the preheated oven and bake for 8–10 minutes. Garnish with chopped parsley and serve.

ROMANA PIZZA
For 2 Romanas you'll need 160g béchamel sauce and 170g mozzarella. The other ingredients stay the same.

AKA the Godfather – quite a name to live up to, but this pizza does it in spades with its riot of colour. The chargrilled veg and passata give a bright Mediterranean base that's perfectly complemented by the chicken and pesto, then tempered with mozzarella. Tearing the chicken by hand instead of chopping with a knife is key here. As the pizza bakes, the chicken, kissed by the pesto, absorbs all the oils and flavours, creating craggy, charred edges that give a wonderful texture.

Il Padrino

MAKES 2 CLASSIC PIZZAS
1 quantity of pizza dough
    (see pages 18–19)
olive oil, for greasing
flour, for dusting
160g passata
160g chargrilled vegetables
    from a jar or roasted
    vegetables (see page 245)
100g cooked chicken
130g block mozzarella, diced
2 pinches dried oregano
freshly ground black pepper
60g (3 heaped tbsp) pesto
    (see page 243 or
    shop-bought)

To finish
24 sunblush tomatoes

1. While your dough is rising, preheat your oven to 230°C/Fan 210°C/ Gas 8. Lightly oil a couple of non-stick baking trays.

2. Dust your work surface with flour. Press and push each piece of dough into a circle about 24cm in diameter. (For more info on working with your dough, see pages 20–21.) Place your pizza bases on the baking trays.

3. Using a tablespoon, spread a thin layer of passata over the pizza bases, taking it almost to the edges. Add the chargrilled or roasted vegetables, spreading them evenly over the pizzas, then tear the chicken into pieces and add them too. Sprinkle over the mozzarella and season with oregano and black pepper. Drizzle the pesto over both pizzas.

4. Place the pizzas in the preheated oven and bake for 8–10 minutes. Dot the sunblush tomatoes over the pizzas, then serve.

ROMANA PIZZA
For 2 Romanas you'll need 170g mozzarella. The other ingredients stay the same.

Boxing Day flavours on a pizza! This is a great example of how well salty pork or gammon can work with sweet and tangy fruit. Chutney concentrates and intensifies the flavour of fruit and enlivens it with the sharp kick of vinegar, and the goat's cheese adds a deep savoury note that brings everything together. Use whatever apricot chutney you like best, but be sure not to go with apricot jam by mistake. It would be much too sweet and would burn in the oven.

Maple-Glazed Gammon

MAKES 2 CLASSIC PIZZAS
1 quantity of pizza dough
   (see pages 18-19)
olive oil, for greasing
flour, for dusting
160g passata
60g apricot chutney
100g maple-glazed ham hock
   (see page 249)
1 slice (45g) goat's cheese
70g block mozzarella, diced
2 pinches dried oregano
freshly ground black pepper
2 dessertspoons garlic oil

To finish
10g Parmesan cheese, grated
chopped parsley

1. While your dough is rising, preheat your oven to 230°C/Fan 210°C/ Gas 8. Lightly oil a couple of non-stick baking trays.

2. Dust your work surface with flour. Press and push each piece of dough into a circle about 24cm in diameter. (For more info on working with your dough, see pages 20–21.) Place your pizza bases on the baking trays.

3. Using a tablespoon, spread a thin layer of passata over the pizza bases, taking it almost to the edges. Add dollops of chutney on each pizza, then pieces of the ham hock, dividing it evenly between the pizzas. Crumble over the goat's cheese and add the mozzarella. Season with oregano and pepper, then drizzle a spoonful of garlic oil over each pizza.

4. Place the pizzas in the preheated oven and bake for 8–10 minutes. Sprinkle over the grated Parmesan and chopped parsley, then serve.

ROMANA PIZZA
For 2 Romanas you'll need 80g apricot chutney, 140g maple-glazed ham hock, 2 slices (90g) goat's cheese, 90g mozzarella and 20g Parmesan. The other ingredients stay the same.

Porchetta is the ultimate Italian feast for high days and holidays, so it's no surprise that this pizza often appears on our Christmas menu. Traditionally, porchetta is a whole boned pig, seasoned with fennel and roasted in a wood-fired oven, but it can also be a smaller joint of pork, roasted with fennel seeds and other aromatics. It's the real star of the show here – a feast of meltingly soft and delicious meat – but there's a multitude of supporting acts that enhance its unctuous texture and flavour.

Porchetta

MAKES 2 CLASSIC PIZZAS
1 quantity of pizza dough
    (see pages 18–19)
olive oil, for greasing
120g new potatoes, scrubbed
flour, for dusting
100g béchamel sauce
    (see page 242)
2 pinches dried or chopped
    fresh sage
100g pulled porchetta
    (see page 247)
6 slices (60g) pancetta
130g block mozzarella, diced
freshly ground black pepper

To finish
20g Parmesan cheese, grated

1. While your dough is rising, preheat your oven to 230°C/Fan 210°C/Gas 8. Lightly oil a couple of non-stick baking trays.

2. Cook the potatoes in a pan of salted water until tender, then drain, slice thinly and set aside.

3. Dust your work surface with flour. Press and push each piece of dough into a circle about 24cm in diameter. (For more info on working with your dough, see pages 20–21.) Place your pizza bases on the baking trays.

4. Using a tablespoon, spread a thin layer of béchamel over the pizza bases, taking it almost to the edges. Sprinkle the bases with sage and add the potato slices. Tear the pulled porchetta into small pieces and divide them evenly between the pizzas. Tear each slice of pancetta into 3 and add these, then scatter over the mozzarella. Season with black pepper.

5. Place the pizzas in the preheated oven and bake for 8–10 minutes. Finish with grated Parmesan.

ROMANA PIZZA
For 2 Romanas you'll need 160g béchamel sauce, 160g pulled porchetta, 170g mozzarella. The other ingredients stay the same.

Sausage and friarelli is a classic combination, traditionally enjoyed in Naples during the winter months. Commonly used in both pasta dishes and pizza, friarelli is an Italian green vegetable that's known by several other names, such as rapini or cime di rapa. It makes an ideal partner for sausage, its savoury, slightly bitter flavour contrasting beautifully with the sweetness of the pork. If you struggle to find friarelli, tenderstem broccoli is a good substitute. It doesn't have quite the same bitter edge but will still be delicious – just make sure you slice the stems thinly. Choose a good Italian sausage with plenty of fennel and herbs.

Campana

MAKES 2 CLASSIC PIZZAS
1 quantity of pizza dough
    (see pages 18–19)
olive oil, for greasing
flour, for dusting
160g passata
120g Italian fennel sausage
100g friarelli or
    tenderstem broccoli
130g block mozzarella, diced
10g Parmesan cheese, grated
2 pinches dried oregano
freshly ground black pepper
2 dessertspoons garlic oil

To finish
10g Parmesan cheese, grated
chopped parsley

1. While your dough is rising, preheat your oven to 230°C/Fan 210°C/Gas 8. Lightly oil a couple of non-stick baking trays.

2. Dust your work surface with flour. Press and push each piece of dough into a circle about 24cm in diameter. (For more info on working with your dough, see pages 20–21.) Place your pizza bases on the baking trays.

3. Using a tablespoon, spread a thin layer of passata over the pizza bases, taking it almost to the edges. Crumble over the sausage, dividing it equally between the pizzas, then add the friarelli, tearing it into small pieces, or broccoli, if using. Add the mozzarella and Parmesan, then season with oregano and black pepper. Drizzle a spoonful of garlic oil over each pizza.

4. Place the pizzas in the preheated oven and bake for 8–10 minutes. Finish with grated Parmesan and chopped parsley, then serve.

ROMANA PIZZA
For 2 Romanas you'll need 160g crumbled sausage, 170g mozzarella, 20g Parmesan and another 20g to finish. The other ingredients stay the same.

This is definitely cold weather food. Inspired by the cooking in the very north of Italy, this recipe includes speck, which is a dry-cured ham produced in the region. Similar in cut and cure to prosciutto, it is then lightly smoked. That smoky flavour does work so well in this recipe, so if you can't find speck, look for another smoked ham. This pizza also features fontal cheese, a semi-soft cow's milk cheese that melts beautifully and has a mild, nutty, slightly sweet taste. The finishing touch is provided by three types of mushroom to enrich the pizza and warm you up on a cold day.

Al Tirolo

MAKES 2 CLASSIC PIZZAS
1 quantity of pizza dough
    (see pages 18–19)
olive oil, for greasing
flour, for dusting
160g passata
30g cup mushrooms,
    wiped and sliced
40g porcini mushrooms,
    soaked in warm water
    for 10–15 minutes
30g portobello mushrooms,
    wiped and sliced
130g fontal cheese, diced
2 tsp garlic oil
freshly ground black pepper
4 slices (60g) speck

To finish
chopped parsley

1. While your dough is rising, preheat your oven to 230°C/Fan 210°C/Gas 8. Lightly oil a couple of non-stick baking trays.

2. Dust your work surface with flour. Press and push each piece of dough into a circle about 24cm in diameter. (For more info on working with your dough, see pages 20–21.) Place your pizza bases on the baking trays.

3. Using a tablespoon, spread a thin layer of passata over the pizza bases, taking it almost to the edges. Scatter the cup mushrooms over the bases. Squeeze the dried mushrooms to remove excess liquid, then add them along with the portobello mushrooms, dividing both equally between the pizzas. Scatter over the cheese and drizzle each pizza with a teaspoon of garlic oil. Season with black pepper

4. Place the pizzas in the preheated oven and bake for 4–5 minutes. Remove and add the speck, torn into pieces. Put the pizzas back in the oven and cook for another 4–5 minutes. Garnish with chopped parsley before serving.

ROMANA PIZZA
For 2 Romanas you'll need 50g cup mushrooms, 60g porcini mushrooms, 50g portobello mushrooms and 170g fontal cheese. The other ingredients stay the same.

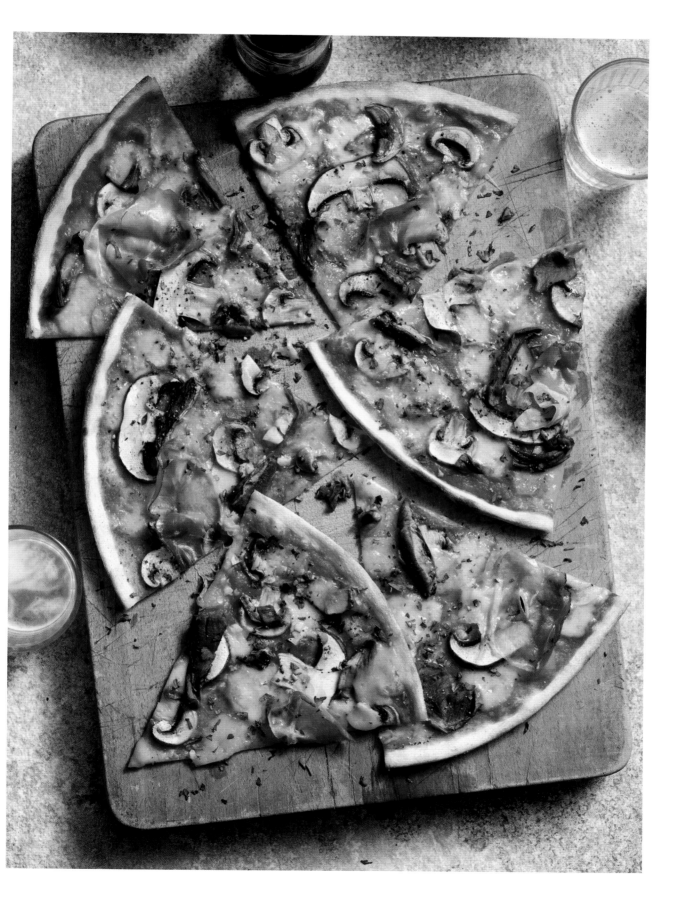

MAKES 2 CLASSIC PIZZAS
1 quantity of pizza dough
   (see pages 18–19)
olive oil, for greasing
flour, for dusting
100g béchamel sauce
   (see page 242)
12 black olives, pitted
60g chestnut mushrooms,
   wiped and sliced
120g maple-glazed ham hock
   (see page 249)
1 x 125g ball of buffalo
   mozzarella, drained
2 pinches dried oregano
freshly ground black pepper
2 dessertspoons garlic oil

To finish
2 dessertspoons truffle oil
chopped parsley

Created as part of our Romana '65 range to celebrate fifty years of PizzaExpress, La Regina is a more indulgent version of our classic La Reine recipe. This pizza features buffalo mozzarella, chestnut mushrooms and shredded ham hock to create a great texture and give a good meaty bite. A drizzle of truffle oil as a finishing touch confirms its truly royal credentials.

La Regina

1. While your dough is rising, preheat your oven to 230°C/Fan 210°C/ Gas 8. Lightly oil a couple of non-stick baking trays.

2. Dust your work surface with flour. Press and push each piece of dough into a circle about 24cm in diameter. (For more info on working with your dough, see pages 20–21.) Place your pizza bases on the baking trays.

3. Using a tablespoon, spread the béchamel over the pizza bases, taking it almost to the edges. Arrange 6 olives around the edge of each pizza. Add the chestnut mushrooms, then shred the ham hock and scatter over the bases. Tear the mozzarella into pieces and divide between the pizzas. Season with oregano and black pepper, and drizzle a spoonful of garlic oil over each pizza.

4. Place the pizzas in the preheated oven and bake for 8–10 minutes. Drizzle each one with a spoonful of truffle oil, sprinkle with parsley, then serve.

ROMANA PIZZA
For 2 Romanas you'll need 160g béchamel sauce, 16 black olives and 160g maple-glazed ham hock. The other ingredients stay the same.

MAKES 2 CLASSIC PIZZAS
1 quantity of pizza dough
 (see pages 18–19)
olive oil, for greasing
flour, for dusting
160g passata
60g chestnut mushrooms,
 wiped and sliced
80g Brussels sprouts,
 trimmed and thinly sliced
1 small red onion, peeled
 and thinly sliced
130g block mozzarella, diced
2 pinches dried oregano
freshly ground black pepper
2 dessertspoons garlic oil
1 tsp pine kernels
6 slices (60g) pancetta
2 free-range eggs

To finish
20g Parmesan cheese shavings
chopped parsley

Most dishes taste better with pancetta and, whether you love them or hate them, Brussels sprouts definitely fall into this category. The nutty sweetness of this festive staple pairs brilliantly with the crisp pancetta, crunch of pine kernels and rich egg. Make sure you slice the sprouts into nice thin slivers so they cook through, and don't forget to add garlic oil to lift all the flavours.

Sprout & Pancetta

1. While your dough is rising, preheat your oven to 230°C/Fan 210°C/Gas 8. Lightly oil a couple of non-stick baking trays.

2. Dust your work surface with flour. Press and push each piece of dough into a circle about 24cm in diameter. (For more info on working with your dough, see pages 20–21.) Place your pizza bases on the baking trays.

3. Using a tablespoon, spread a thin layer of passata over the pizza bases, taking it almost to the edges. Leaving a space in the middle of each pizza for the egg, arrange the mushroom, sprout and onion slices evenly over the pizzas. Scatter over the mozzarella, again leaving space in the centre, then season with oregano and black pepper. Drizzle each pizza with a spoonful of garlic oil and sprinkle over the pine kernels.

4. Arrange the pancetta slices around the space at the centre of each pizza. If you prefer your eggs cooked through, crack an egg into the centre of each pizza, place them in the preheated oven and bake for 8–10 minutes. If you prefer soft eggs, cook the pizzas for 4–5 minutes first, then add the eggs and cook for another 4–5 minutes.

5. Add the Parmesan shavings, then sprinkle with chopped parsley and serve.

ROMANA PIZZA
For 2 Romanas you'll need 140g Brussels sprouts, 170g mozzarella and 8 slices (80g) pancetta. The other ingredients stay the same.

This fresh, vibrant pizza is all about the final flourishes, so make sure that everyone is sitting down and ready to enjoy it at its best. The Rustichella (pronounced roost-ee-keh-la) disappeared from the menu for a while, but in 2016 a loyal customer and avid fan campaigned for its return. We had to oblige. Even though it is not listed at the moment, fans can still enjoy it in the restaurants, as the ingredients are always available. Our motto is: if we have the ingredients to make a Heritage recipe we absolutely will.

Rustichella

MAKES 2 CLASSIC PIZZAS
1 quantity of pizza dough
   (see pages 18–19)
olive oil, for greasing
flour, for dusting
160g passata
6 slices (60g) pancetta
130g block mozzarella, diced
2 pinches dried oregano

To finish
handful of rocket leaves
16 sunblush tomatoes
60ml Caesar dressing
   (see page 244 or
   shop-bought)
30g Parmesan cheese shavings

1. While your dough is rising, preheat your oven to 230°C/Fan 210°C/ Gas 8. Lightly oil a couple of non-stick baking trays.

2. Dust your work surface with flour. Press and push each piece of dough into a circle about 24cm in diameter. (For more info on working with your dough, see pages 20–21.) Place your pizza bases on the baking trays.

3. Using a tablespoon, spread a thin layer of passata over the pizza bases, taking it almost to the edges. Tear each slice of pancetta into 3 pieces and add these to the pizzas, spreading them evenly. Add the mozzarella and season with oregano.

4. Place the pizzas in the preheated oven and bake for 8–10 minutes. Scatter rocket leaves over the pizzas, then add the sunblush tomatoes. Drizzle the dressing over the rocket and tomatoes, then add the Parmesan shavings and serve.

ROMANA PIZZA
For 2 Romanas you'll need 10 slices (100g) pancetta, 170g mozzarella and a large handful of rocket leaves. The other ingredients stay the same.

The Ragù has a base of rich ragù sauce instead of passata, so that meaty flavour is in every bite. Plenty of robust herbs and seasoning go into this recipe, and the addition of ricotta, a rich but mild cheese, keeps it beautifully mellow. Ricotta starts life as the whey from the production of mozzarella or other cheese. It is then cooked for a second time (hence its name which means 'recooked') to produce creamy curds that are used in both sweet and savoury dishes.

Ragù

MAKES 2 CLASSIC PIZZAS
1 quantity of pizza dough
(see pages 18–19)
olive oil, for greasing
flour, for dusting
100g ragù sauce (see page 222)
1 small red onion, peeled
and thinly sliced
50g ricotta
70g block mozzarella, diced
2 pinches fennel seeds
2 pinches dried oregano
2 pinches dried or chopped
fresh rosemary
freshly ground black pepper
2 dessertspoons garlic oil

To finish
16 sunblush tomatoes
30g Parmesan cheese shavings
chopped parsley

1. While your dough is rising, preheat your oven to 230°C/Fan 210°C/Gas 8. Lightly oil a couple of non-stick baking trays.

2. Dust your work surface with flour. Press and push each piece of dough into a circle about 24cm in diameter. (For more info on working with your dough, see pages 20–21.) Place your pizza bases on the baking trays.

3. Using a tablespoon, spread a layer of ragù over the pizza bases, taking it almost to the edges. Add the slices of red onion, then dollops of ricotta, dividing them equally between each pizza. Add the mozzarella, then season with fennel seeds, oregano, rosemary and black pepper. Drizzle a spoonful of garlic oil over each pizza.

4. Place the pizzas in the preheated oven and bake for 8–10 minutes. Add the sunblush tomatoes and Parmesan shavings, sprinkle with chopped parsley and serve.

ROMANA PIZZA
For 2 Romanas you'll need 100g ricotta and 90g mozzarella. The other ingredients stay the same.

Roast beef, horseradish and potatoes – Sunday dinner on a pizza! The beef is definitely the hero ingredient on this pizza, and its rich flavour is brought out by the horseradish. Always make sure you break up any bigger chunks of beef and spread the meat and potatoes evenly over the pizzas so you get the perfect mix of taste and texture each time. We've included just the right amount of horseradish for a good balance, but for those super-fans who like this condiment to be nose-tinglingly strong, serve some extra on the side.

Beef & Horseradish

MAKES 2 CLASSIC PIZZAS
1 quantity of pizza dough
  (see pages 18–19)
olive oil, for greasing
100g new potatoes, scrubbed
flour, for dusting
160g passata
1 small red onion,
  peeled and sliced
100g beef, diced and mixed
  with 2 tsp horseradish sauce
130g block mozzarella, diced
2 pinches dried oregano
1 tsp finely chopped rosemary
freshly ground black pepper
2 dessertspoons garlic oil

To finish
10g Parmesan cheese, grated
chopped parsley

1. While your dough is rising, preheat your oven to 230°C/Fan 210°C/Gas 8. Lightly oil a couple of non-stick baking trays.

2. Cook the potatoes in a pan of salted water until tender, then drain, slice thinly and set aside.

3. Dust your work surface with flour. Press and push each piece of dough into a circle about 24cm in diameter. (For more info on working with your dough, see pages 20–21.) Place your pizza bases on the baking trays.

4. Using a tablespoon, spread a thin layer of passata over the pizza bases, taking it almost to the edges. Add the slices of onion and potato. Now add the beef and horseradish, dividing it evenly between the pizzas, and sprinkle over the mozzarella. Season with oregano, rosemary and black pepper. Drizzle each pizza with a spoonful of garlic oil.

5. Place the pizzas in the preheated oven and bake for 8–10 minutes. Finish with grated Parmesan and chopped parsley.

ROMANA PIZZA
For 2 Romanas you'll need 120g potato, 140g beef and 3 tsp horseradish, 170g mozzarella and 20g Parmesan. The other ingredients stay the same.

SALADS &
AL FORNO

As lovely as it would be to eat pizza seven days a week (and trust me, we have tried!), we all need balance in our lives. Sometimes you might fancy something a bit different but with all the wonderful PizzaExpress flavours. Our salads and al forno (oven-baked) pasta dishes are great additions to our menu, and we make sure we have the best recipes.

Salads

Imagine you're sitting at a table and everyone around you is enjoying pizza but you ordered a salad. The last thing you want is to have food envy or feel like you've drawn the short straw. That's why we always put as much effort into making sure every salad recipe is just as tempting and delicious as our pizzas.

Al Forno

Our kitchens are the heart of our pizzerias and we cook everything in our pizza ovens, which are set at 371°C. There are no hobs, fryers or microwaves hiding somewhere at the back – all the food comes from the oven. This can make it tricky to cook anything but pizza. Over the years, we have adapted, tested and trialled many other dishes, and only those that taste great and work in our ovens find their way onto our menu. We're often asked why we don't have spaghetti alla carbonara on our menu. The answer is simple – we can't make a great version in our ovens (yet!), so we don't make one at all, except in pizza form (see page 176).

'Al forno' means 'to the oven' or 'baked', and our Al Forno range features some great dishes that work brilliantly in the fiery heat of our ovens. Lasagne, with its blistered béchamel and cheese top, is truly a feast, and our Pollo Pesto, with morsels of charred chicken and sizzling green pesto, is a real delight. These recipes are just as successful in domestic ovens, and we hope they are as popular around your table as they are around ours.

The classic Italian salad, this is all about using great ingredients. There's no cooking needed, so the salad is perfect for sunny days and meals outside, but it's equally good on drizzly, damp days when you want to let a little sunshine into your kitchen. The colours echo those of the Italian flag – the white of the mozzarella, with its mild, creamy, soft texture, is the perfect counterpart to bright red tomatoes and the herbal hit of green pesto. Great before pizza, with pizza, or just on its own. To get the best flavour from this dish, take the mozzarella and tomatoes out of the fridge a couple of hours before you are going to make your salad to allow time for them to come to room temperature.

SERVES 2
20 baby plum tomatoes, halved
freshly ground black pepper
1 x 125g ball buffalo mozzarella
2 tsp extra virgin olive oil
20g (1 heaped tbsp) pesto
   (see page 243 or
   shop-bought)
basil leaves

Mozzarella & Tomato Salad

1. Divide the tomatoes between your serving plates and season with black pepper.

2. Pull the mozzarella into pieces and scatter them over the tomatoes.

3. Drizzle a teaspoon of oil over each serving, then spoon over some pesto. Garnish with basil leaves, then serve.

With bags of flavour, this recipe is packed with fun, exciting ingredients that will make everyone smile when you tell them what's for dinner. The tomatoes and olives provide that typically Italian base and combine with the savoury tang of goat's cheese, tender chicken and crunchy croutons to make this a real treat. Red chilli pepper pearls add a wonderful pop of flavour, but if you're not a fan of mild spice, you could add slices of red pepper – fresh or from a jar – instead. And if you're veggie, you could leave the chicken out and the salad still tastes great, though it might need a new name!

Pollo Salad

SERVES 2
90ml house dressing
   (see page 245)
160g mixed salad leaves
12 croutons
2 large vine tomatoes,
   each cut into 6 chunks
12 black olives, pitted
200g cooked chicken,
   torn into pieces
90g goat's cheese
28 red chilli pepper pearls
2 dessertspoons extra
   virgin olive oil
freshly ground black pepper

To serve
dough sticks (see page 29)

1. Put a couple of tablespoons of the house dressing into a large salad bowl. Add the mixed leaves, top with croutons, then drizzle over the remaining dressing. Add the tomatoes and olives to the bowl.

2. Add the pieces of chicken and crumble over the goat's cheese, then add the chilli pearls.

3. Drizzle over the extra virgin olive oil and season with black pepper. Serve with dough sticks on the side.

SERVES 2
2 free-range eggs,
  room temperature
90ml Caesar dressing
  (see page 244)
200g cos lettuce,
  torn into pieces
handful of rocket leaves
12 croutons
200g cooked chicken,
  torn into pieces
30g Parmesan cheese shavings
6 white anchovies
20ml extra virgin olive oil
freshly ground black pepper

To serve
chopped parsley
dough sticks (see page 29)

A good Caesar dressing is what makes this salad, and we pride ourselves on making the best dressings. First created by an Italian in North America, this salad epitomises the 'make something out of what you've got' mentality, and – hey presto – the world got something special. Make sure the leaves have a good coating of dressing, so they're creamy and tangy, but don't overdo it or the salad could become soggy. We like to add hard-boiled eggs to our salad (free-range, of course) for extra goodness and texture, and a handful of rocket leaves for a peppery flavour hit.

Grand Chicken Caesar Salad

1. First, hard-boil your eggs. Put the eggs in a pan, cover with cold water and bring to the boil. Simmer for 7 or 8 minutes, then remove and place under cold running water until cool. Peel and set aside.

2. Put 2 tablespoons of Caesar dressing in a large salad bowl. Add the lettuce and rocket leaves, then top with croutons. Drizzle over the remaining dressing.

3. Slice the eggs and add them to the bowl with the chicken. Scatter over the Parmesan shavings and arrange the anchovies on top. Drizzle with extra virgin oil and season with black pepper.

4. Garnish the salad with chopped parsley and serve with the dough sticks on the side.

This may not be an Italian classic – anything with the title Niçoise hails from the French city of Nice – but it is a PizzaExpress classic. First listed in 1985, it includes many of the robust ingredients that are great on pizza and that we continue to use today. Anchovies, capers, olives and tuna bring big flavours and, combined with fresh salad leaves and kissed with our special house dressing, it's not hard to see why this is still on the menu. You'll find white anchovies on deli counters and in fish shops. They are briefly salted, then marinated in vinegar and oil and have a milder flavour than the brown anchovies in tins or jars.

Niçoise Salad

SERVES 2
2 free-range eggs,
   room temperature
90ml house dressing
   (see page 245)
160g mixed salad leaves
2 vine tomatoes,
   each cut into 6 chunks
½ cucumber, sliced
12 black olives, pitted
200g tinned tuna, drained
6 white anchovies
2 tsp capers
2 dessertspoons extra
   virgin olive oil

To serve
chopped parsley
½ lemon, cut into wedges
dough sticks (see page 29)

1. First, hard-boil your eggs. Put the eggs in a pan, cover with cold water and bring to the boil. Simmer for 7 or 8 minutes, then remove and place under cold running water until cool. Peel and set aside.

2. Put 2 tablespoons of house dressing into a large salad bowl. Add the mixed leaves and drizzle with the remaining dressing. Add the tomatoes, cucumber slices and olives.

3. Flake the tuna over the salad and top with the white anchovies, placing them silver-side up, then sprinkle over the capers.

4. Slice the eggs and add them to the bowl, then drizzle the salad with the extra virgin olive oil.

5. Garnish with chopped parsley and lemon wedges, then serve with dough sticks.

By far and away the top seller in our Al Forno range, this has comfort and flavour in one. A rich, creamy béchamel sauce provides the base, but it is the dollops of pesto that make it sing. Earthy mushrooms, torn chicken and a generous helping of cheese bring it all together into a glorious suppertime feast. This is perfect for date night or to enjoy on the sofa as you put your feet up and watch your favourite TV programme. And if you're having friends over, just double up the recipe. If you're veggie, use some roasted cubes of butternut squash or strips of roasted pepper instead of chicken, or simply use double the quantity of mushrooms and vegetarian cheese instead of Parmesan. Just be sure you give everything a good mix before the dish goes into the oven, and if there are any pieces of penne poking through on the surface, push them into the sauce so that they don't get too crisp or burn.

Pollo Pesto Pasta

SERVES 2 GENEROUSLY
400g béchamel sauce
  (see page 242)
200g penne pasta
100g pesto (see page 243
  or shop-bought)
80g cup mushrooms,
  wiped and sliced
1 small red onion,
  peeled and thinly sliced
140g cooked chicken,
  torn into pieces
80g mozzarella, torn or diced
20g Parmesan cheese, grated

To serve
20g Parmesan cheese, grated
basil leaves

1. Make the béchamel sauce and set aside.

2. In a separate pan, cook the pasta in salted boiling water according to the packet instructions, then drain and set aside. Preheat the oven to 200°C/Fan 180°C/Gas 6.

3. Stir the pesto into the béchamel and mix well, then stir in the mushrooms, onion slices, chicken and pasta. Make sure everything is well combined, then spoon into an ovenproof dish and top with the mozzarella and grated Parmesan.

4. Bake in the preheated oven for 20–25 minutes until the pasta is hot all the way through and the cheese has melted. Serve, topped with grated Parmesan and basil leaves.

SERVES 2
250g béchamel sauce
  (see page 242)
7 lasagne sheets
1 x 125g ball of buffalo mozzarella
30g Parmesan cheese, grated

Ragù sauce
50g pancetta, diced
1 tbsp finely chopped red onion
2 garlic cloves, peeled
  and finely chopped
25g unsalted butter
1 tbsp finely chopped carrot
1 tbsp finely chopped celery
1 bay leaf
100g minced beef
100g minced pork
60g cup mushrooms,
  wiped and chopped
½ glass of red wine
400g passata
1 tsp chopped parsley
salt and freshly ground
  black pepper

The ultimate Al Forno dish, lasagne is a comforting mix of slow-cooked meat sauce, silky pasta and creamy béchamel, with a crisp, golden topping of mozzarella and Parmesan. It's perfect get-ahead food – make it in the morning, or the day before you want to eat, and then just pop it in the oven 30–40 minutes before serving. And if you're cooking for a crowd, you can double up the recipe. This is something the whole family will enjoy, served with a simple rocket or tomato salad.

Lasagne

1. First, make the ragù. Place a medium-sized saucepan over a medium heat, add the pancetta and cook until golden brown. Stir in the onion, garlic and butter and cook until the onion is soft, then add the carrot, celery and bay leaf and cook for about 4 minutes. Stir in the beef and pork, breaking it all up with a wooden spoon, and cook until nicely browned. Add the mushrooms and wine and simmer for about 3 minutes.

2. Stir in the passata, add the parsley and season to taste. Cover the pan and simmer for about 45 minutes. Keep an eye on the sauce – you may need to add a little water from time to time to keep it from becoming too dry. Set the sauce aside.

3. Preheat the oven to 180°C/Fan 160°C/Gas 4. Take an ovenproof dish measuring about 15 x 20cm and spread about a third of the meat sauce over the base. Add a layer of 2 lasagne sheets, then spread with a third of the béchamel. Sprinkle with Parmesan cheese.

4. Repeat the layers twice more, breaking up the additional lasagne sheet to fill any gaps. Tear the mozzarella into pieces and add to the top, then sprinkle over the remaining Parmesan.

5. Place the dish in the preheated oven and bake for 30–40 minutes until the lasagne is bubbling and the top is beautifully brown.

This is not so much a vegan pasta recipe, but rather a delicious pasta dish that happens to be vegan. Big flavours from chilli, garlic and rosemary work so well with the passata and the smoky, roasted peppers to create a full-bodied sauce that packs a punch. It's quick to put together, so a great dish for when you need to get something on the table quickly. In the restaurant we bake this in the oven, but we've tweaked the recipe so it can be cooked on the hob. Penne pasta is ideal, and you can always substitute it with a gluten-free version if you prefer.

SERVES 2
40ml garlic oil
240g passata
200g roasted peppers
   from a jar, sliced
1 tbsp chopped parsley
½ tsp chopped rosemary
2 pinches chilli flakes
200g penne pasta

To serve
handful of rocket leaves
chopped parsley

Peperonata Pasta

1. Pour the garlic oil into a pan and add the passata, roasted peppers, parsley, rosemary and chilli flakes. Stir well and leave to simmer for 8–10 minutes.

2. Meanwhile, bring a large pan of salted water to the boil, add the pasta and cook according to the packet instructions. When the pasta is done, drain it, reserving a couple of spoonfuls of the cooking water.

3. Add the pasta and the reserved cooking water to the pan of sauce and cook for a couple of minutes. Serve garnished with rocket and parsley.

DESSERTS

Do you crave a little something sweet after your pizza? Dessert is the finale to a meal, so really needs to shine. If it's average, you might not bother again, but if it's perfect you'll dream about it! Whether you go chocolatey, creamy or fruity, dessert success is about getting the right balance – sweet, but not too sweet, generous, but not over the top, and just the right level of indulgence so you feel satisfied rather than guilty.

Gelato was the mainstay of our dessert selection for many years, whether simply as a variety of flavours or in a different guise, such as a bombe, tartufo or affogato. And from 1965 to 1990 we also listed a savoury end to the meal: cheese and biscuits. But something happened in 1982 that changed everything … chocolate fudge cake. Made in-house, this was a game-changer. Before then, desserts did not even have their own section on our menu, there were just a couple of options sitting quietly at the bottom. From 1983 onwards, desserts increased in prominence, with their own heading, and exciting new options joined the menu.

While chocolate fudge cake and gelato remain staples, we have developed our range over the years, and we enjoy being more playful and trying out something a bit different. Adding new flavours and ingredients, along with the traditional, ensures that we always have something exciting for you to enjoy.

Sometimes you just want a little touch of sweetness, so we created our Dolcetti range, mini desserts enjoyed with an espresso – or whatever hot drink you like. It's easy to create these at home by serving half portions on a smaller dish and some coffee on the side. Or you can save on the washing up and share one dessert between two. Whatever dessert mood you are in, a little bit of what you fancy can be a good thing.

The name of this Italian classic translates as 'pick-me up' and refers to the coffee in which the ladyfingers are dipped. With its flavours of dark cocoa, strong coffee and sweet booze, together with creamy mascarpone, this is one that keeps the party going. If you're serving more people – or you just love tiramisu – you can double or triple the ingredients.

SERVES 2 HUNGRY PEOPLE
1 large free-range egg yolk
10g caster sugar
30g mascarpone
150ml double cream
60ml espresso coffee
30ml sweet Marsala wine
    or coffee liqueur
    (Tia Maria)
15–20 Savoiardi sponge
    finger biscuits
cocoa powder, for dusting

Tiramisu

1. In a large bowl, whisk the egg yolk and sugar together with an electric whisk until pale and creamy. Stir the mascarpone into the egg mixture until well combined.

2. In a separate bowl, whip the double cream until soft peaks form. With a metal spoon, fold the whipped cream into the mascarpone mixture.

3. Mix the espresso and Marsala together in a shallow bowl. Dip half of the biscuits into the mixture, then lay them flat in a serving dish, measuring about 15 x 20cm. (Don't try to dip all the biscuits at once or they will get too soggy.)

4. Spoon half the mascarpone mix over the biscuits. Dip the remaining biscuits and place them on top of the mascarpone mix, then spoon over the remaining mascarpone. Cover and chill in the fridge for 24 hours. Dust with cocoa powder before serving.

SERVES 8
80ml olive oil, plus
extra for greasing
130g plain flour
40g cocoa powder
1 tsp baking powder
1 tsp bicarbonate of soda
½ tsp salt
240g golden caster sugar
40g golden syrup
80ml buttermilk
2 large free-range eggs,
lightly beaten

Fudge icing
250g good-quality dark
chocolate, broken
into pieces
250g unsalted butter,
room temperature
225g icing sugar
20g cornflour
1 tsp vanilla extract

Walking into one of our restaurants as a freshly baked chocolate fudge cake is taken out of the oven to cool is always a delight – and the cake is even better when iced and ready to eat with a big scoop of vanilla gelato on the side. We only have a pizza oven to cook in, so chocolate fudge cake is always the first item baked each day while the oven is still at a low temperature. Once cooled, it is adorned with lashings of chocolate fudge icing – pure chocolatey goodness.

Chocolate Fudge Cake

1. Grease the base of two 18cm sandwich tins with a little oil and line with baking paper. Preheat the oven to 180°C/Fan 160°C/Gas 4.

2. Sift the flour, cocoa powder, salt, baking powder and bicarbonate of soda into a bowl. Add the caster sugar and mix well. Make a well in the centre and add the golden syrup, olive oil, buttermilk, eggs and 80ml of water. Beat well with an electric whisk until smooth.

3. Pour the mixture into the prepared tins and bake for 25–30 minutes until the cakes have risen and are firm to the touch. Remove from the oven and leave to cool for 10 minutes, then carefully turn the cakes out onto a cooling rack.

4. For the icing, put the chocolate into a heatproof bowl and place it over a pan of barely simmering water. The bottom of the bowl shouldn't touch the water. Allow the chocolate to melt, stirring occasionally. Set the chocolate aside to cool slightly.

5. Beat the butter in a bowl until soft. Gradually sift and beat in the icing sugar and cornflour, then add the cooled chocolate and the vanilla extract. Mix thoroughly until smooth and glossy.

6. Once the sponges have cooled to room temperature, spread half the fudge icing over one of the sponges, then place the second one on top. Spread the remaining icing on top and swirl it attractively to the edges. Cut into slices to serve, with some or pouring cream if you like. If you feel really adventurous, cut each sponge in half horizontally, so you have 4 layers to sandwich together with icing.

MAKES 8
200g unsalted butter, diced
210g good-quality dark
   chocolate, broken into pieces
5 medium free-range eggs
200g golden caster sugar
50g cocoa powder
150g plain flour

For coating the ramekins
50g butter, melted
cocoa powder, for dusting

If you like chocolate, chances are you are a fan of the chocolate fondant, which represents all that's right in the chocolate world. The cooking time is key here, as the outside must be cooked while the inside remains an ooze of chocolate loveliness. You will need eight ramekins with a diameter of about 8cm.

Chocolate Fondant Puddings

1. First, prepare the ramekins so that the puddings don't stick when you turn them out. Using a pastry brush, coat the inside of each ramekin with the melted butter. Add some cocoa powder and tip the ramekin until the inside is nicely coated. Preheat the oven to 200°C/Fan 180°C/Gas 6.

2. Place a heatproof bowl over a pan of barely simmering water and add the diced butter and the chocolate. The bottom of the bowl shouldn't touch the water. Allow to melt, then carefully remove the bowl and stir the butter and chocolate together until smooth and combined. Set aside to cool slightly.

3. Crack the eggs into a separate bowl and add the sugar. Using an electric whisk, beat until the mixture is thick and pale. When the mixture is ready, the whisk should leave a little trail when you remove it. Add the melted chocolate and butter to the eggs and sugar and stir gently until velvety smooth.

4. Stir the cocoa powder into the flour, then gently fold them into the wet mixture. Make sure there are no lumps of flour or cocoa powder remaining.

5. Divide the mixture between the prepared moulds and gently tap them to level the contents. Place the ramekins on a baking tray and cook for 10–12 minutes until a crust has formed on the top and the fondants are starting to come away from the sides of the moulds. Remove them from the oven and leave to sit for 1 minute before turning out – if you prefer, you can serve them in the ramekins.

6. Carefully run the tip of a small knife between the sponge and the mould, then turn the puddings out onto plates. Serve at once with cream or ice cream.

Dusted with icing sugar and cinnamon, the classic Christmassy spice, this is a simple recipe but one that's sure to delight. Cinnamon is quite a strong flavour, so if you are not a fan, just leave it out or serve on the side. Go with whatever sauce you like – we use vanilla, salted caramel and fruit coulis in the restaurant, all of which you can buy good versions of in the supermarket. If you prefer something different, chocolate and hazelnut works a treat, or try lemon curd, or even just a scoop of vanilla gelato.

MAKES 16 (SERVES 2)
1 quantity of bread dough
   (see page 26)
flour, for dusting
olive oil, for greasing
cinnamon, for dusting
icing sugar, for dusting

To serve
vanilla-flavoured dip
   with chocolate straws
salted caramel sauce
fruit coulis

Snowball Dough Balls

1. When the dough is ready, generously dust your work surface with flour and lightly oil a baking tray. Shape the dough into a tube and roll it back and forth until it is about 46cm long.

2. Cut this tube in half, then keep cutting the pieces of dough in half until you have 16 even-sized slices. Place these on the baking tray, cover with cling film and leave to prove for 30 minutes. (For more info on preparing your dough balls for baking, see page 27.)

3. Preheat the oven to 230°C/Fan 210°C/Gas 8.

4. Bake the dough balls in the preheated oven for 6 minutes. Leave to cool slightly, then dust lightly with cinnamon and icing sugar.

5. Serve with ramekins of vanilla-flavoured dip, salted caramel sauce and fruit coulis.

SAUCES, DRESSINGS & TOPPINGS

Sauces play a serious role in the pizza game. Whether used for dipping, drizzling, spreading or dressing, they will be in every bite you take, so really have to enhance the dish and work with all the flavours. They also offer a great way to personalise your dish and cater for every taste. Those who like their food extra spicy will love hot jalapeño salsa (see page 243), while others who prefer something a little milder can indulge in a double dip of garlic butter (see page 242). Play around, see what you like best and make it your own.

Dressings are also very important to us at PizzaExpress and we are especially proud of our house dressing. You can enjoy it in our pizzerias, buy it in the supermarket or make your own (see page 245). We know that when you love it, you really love it, so we will always happily give customers extra dressing when dining in. It's our own fault really, for making it too good!

The vast majority of our pizzas are built on a base of delicious passata, but sometimes we like to do something different. We have pizzas with a base of creamy béchamel sauce and a few that feature beautiful butternut squash or sweet potato purée, and you'll find the recipes for those in this chapter. We also like to use roasted vegetables, bringing a blast of Mediterranean flavours to your pizza.

Slow-cooked meats are a great topping for pizzas, as they stay moist and are full of robust flavours. Many need to be cooked for about five hours and are best prepared the day before you want to use them. But this does not mean you're toiling away for hours – there's just a bit of prep and then you can leave the oven to do the hard work. You'll have the satisfaction of knowing you are going to have something delicious to eat and your kitchen will smell totally amazing.

When slow cooking meat, it is so important to use the right cut. If you tried to cook a chicken breast or fillet steak for five hours, even at a low temperature, they would be completely dry and inedible because they are so lean. This is where the less well-known cuts with a good bit of fat come into their own, such as pork shoulder, shin of beef or ham hock. Fat equals flavour and it dissolves as the meat cooks, creating something truly delicious. The bonus of these tasty meats is that they are cheaper than prime lean cuts, such as fillet steak. You should be able to find them in the supermarket or, better still, go to your local butcher. They are the meat experts, so tell them what you want to cook and ask their advice. They will be happy to share their knowledge.

Once the meat is done, you should be able to pull it apart with two forks. Just hold the meat steady with one fork, then use the other to comb the meat towards you. This will give you great shreds and create maximum surface area, so when you put the meat back into the juices it will absorb them all.

With all these slow-cooked meat recipes you will have more than you need for a couple of pizzas. We've suggested a few ways of using leftovers, or you can simply freeze them until you're ready for your next delicious meaty pizza fix!

Garlic Butter

Like fish and chips or salt and vinegar, dough balls and garlic butter just belong together. This is our most popular dip by far. Just two things to remember: first, be sure to have your butter at room temperature so the garlic mixes through properly. And second, use salted butter and don't add extra salt. If you're a fan of garlic butter, it's worth making a large quantity like this. You can divide it into portions and pop it in the freezer to use whenever you like.

MAKES ABOUT 140G
15g garlic cloves, peeled and crushed
1 tsp olive oil
125g salted butter, room temperature

1. Mix the garlic and olive oil together to make a paste. Pour this over the softened butter, then mix well to blend.

Béchamel Sauce

Some of our pizzas have a base of béchamel instead of passata, and this is a great recipe to have in your repertoire. It's perfect for our pizzas and pasta dishes, but you can also use it in a fish pie, as the base for a great cheese sauce, or stir in some fresh parsley and serve it with any leftover maple-glazed ham hock (see page 249).

MAKES ABOUT 250ML
250ml whole milk
½ white onion, peeled
25g salted butter
25g plain flour

1. Pour the milk into a pan, add the onion and heat until the milk is just coming to the boil. Turn off the heat and leave the milk to infuse for about 20 minutes, then remove the onion and discard.

2. Melt the butter in a heavy-bottomed pan, then add the flour. Stir it well over a low heat to cook the flour and form a paste (called a roux). When the roux starts to come away from the side of the pan, it's ready for you to start adding the milk.

3. Add the milk, a little at a time, stirring constantly as the sauce thickens. Keep stirring for 5–10 minutes to make a smooth, thick sauce, then remove the pan from the heat. If you're not using the sauce right away, cover the surface with a piece of cling film to stop a skin forming.

Hot Jalapeño Salsa

Some like it hot, some like it really hot – and they enjoy hot jalapeño salsa. This fiery blend is not only about heat, it also allows the fruitiness of the chillies to come through. It's a great vegan/dairy-free sauce.

MAKES ABOUT 150G
50ml olive oil
50g red chilli peppers from a jar
50g jalapeños from a jar
1 tsp smoky chilli powder

1. Measure the oil into a jug and add the drained red chilli peppers and jalapeños, followed by the chilli powder.

2. Blitz with a hand blender until the mixture is well combined but with pieces of pepper still visible. Don't over blitz, as you want to keep some texture. Store in the fridge for up to 3 days.

Bruschetta Mix

Bruschetta mix adds a bright freshness to any dish. Make sure to dice the tomatoes and onions finely and to a similar size – you don't want to bite down on a big chunk of raw onion.

SERVES 2
140g vine tomatoes, diced
30g red onion, peeled and diced
freshly ground black pepper

1. Put the tomato and onion in a bowl and season with black pepper. Mix thoroughly.

Italian Tomato Dip

So simple but so full of flavour, this dip is great hot or cold.

MAKES ABOUT 400G
400g passata
5–6 garlic cloves, peeled and crushed
10 basil leaves

1. Put the passata into a bowl and add the crushed garlic and basil leaves.

2. Using a hand blender, blitz until the garlic and basil are incorporated and the mixture has become thicker and lighter in colour. Store in the fridge for up to 3 days.

Peter's Pesto

This was Peter's favourite pesto recipe and while it has been tweaked over the years, the addition of butter for richness is still a key twist. Make sure you have plenty of lovely fresh basil and taste the pesto before you season it as the cheese will add a salty edge.

MAKES 170G
30g basil leaves
1 heaped tbsp pine kernels
25g Parmesan or vegetarian
   parmesan-style cheese, grated
80ml extra virgin olive oil
½ garlic clove, peeled and finely chopped
1 tbsp unsalted butter, room temperature
salt and freshly ground black pepper

1. Place all the ingredients in a food processor and blend to make a paste. Taste and add seasoning as required.

2. Spoon into a bowl and, if not using straight away, cover and store in the fridge for up to 3 days.

Red Pesto Sauce

If you find pesto on its own a bit too rich or you're looking for a different option, adding a few spoonfuls to passata is a great way to get maximum flavour with minimum effort. This sauce is good on pizza, pasta or with plain grilled chicken or fish, so is a great one to keep on hand for a fuss-free weeknight dinner.

MAKES ABOUT 320G
80g pesto (see page 243 or shop-bought)
240g passata

1. Put the pesto in a bowl and add the passata. Mix together until thoroughly combined. If not using straight away, cover and store in the fridge for up to 3 days.

Caesar Dressing

Our classic Caesar dressing is all about big, punchy, unapologetic flavours that work with a salad but can also stand up to a Rustichella pizza. Even if you think you're not an anchovy fan, please do give them a try in this recipe (see page 202), as they add a deep savoury flavour.

MAKES 200ML
25g anchovies in oil, drained
2 garlic cloves, peeled and roughly chopped
3 large free-range egg yolks
1 tsp Dijon mustard
2 tbsp lemon juice
60ml vegetable oil
60ml rapeseed oil
2 tbsp finely grated Parmesan cheese
freshly ground black pepper

1. Put the anchovies, garlic, egg yolks, mustard and lemon juice in a food processor and blitz until combined.

2. With the processor running, slowly add the oils, a little at a time, and the mixture will emulsify. Add the Parmesan and a good grind of pepper, then give the dressing a final blitz. This makes a fairly thick dressing, but if you want it thinner, stir through a little water until you reach the consistency you like.

House Dressing

We call this a dressing but really it is so much more. Not only is it amazing on our Pollo and Niçoise salads (see pages 214 and 218), it's also great as a dip for dough balls, chicken wings and pizza crusts, or even for drizzling over pizza. Everyone has their own way to enjoy our house dressing and that's just fine – what will yours be?

MAKES 200ML
1 free-range egg yolk
1 tsp caster sugar
½ tsp salt
freshly ground black pepper
1 tsp Dijon mustard
1 tsp brandy
½ tsp Worcestershire sauce
150ml olive oil
5 tbsp white wine vinegar
lemon juice (optional)
dried oregano
chopped parsley

1. Whisk the egg yolk in a bowl until creamy. Add the sugar, salt, a grind or two of pepper, mustard, brandy and Worcestershire sauce and whisk until the mixture thickens.

2. Now start adding the oil, slowly at first, then more quickly, whisking all the time.

3. Add the vinegar, then taste and add more sugar or salt as needed. If the dressing is greasy but tastes strongly of vinegar, add a little lemon juice. If it is too thick and won't pour easily, add some water.

4. Finally, add a pinch or two of oregano and some chopped parsley.

Balsamic Dressing

We like to keep ours simple – just equal quantities of delicious extra virgin olive oil and rich balsamic vinegar. That's all you need.

MAKES 100ML
50ml extra virgin olive oil
50ml balsamic vinegar

1. Pour the oil into a jug, add the vinegar and whisk to combine.

Roasted Vegetables

These make a lovely topping for pizzas such as our Roasted Veg and Ricotta recipe (see page 98). They're nice by themselves too, with some couscous or salad.

MAKES ABOUT 260G
½ aubergine, cut into chunks
½ courgette, thickly sliced
½ red pepper, deseeded and thickly sliced
½ yellow pepper, deseeded and thickly sliced
20ml garlic oil
3 or 4 thyme sprigs
salt and freshly ground black pepper

1. Preheat the oven to 200°C/Fan 180°C/Gas 6.

2. Put all the vegetables in a roasting tin, drizzle with the oil and toss until everything is nicely coated. Add the thyme sprigs and season with salt and freshly ground black pepper.

3. Roast for 20–25 minutes, turning the vegetables halfway through the cooking time. Check that the vegetables are tender – if not, cook for a few more minutes. Leave to cool before using on your pizza.

Roasted Aubergine

We often use chargrilled aubergine slices – available in jars – on our pizzas, but sometimes we like to add delicious chunks of roasted aubergine. Try these on recipes such as Caponata (see page 117), Vegan Mezze (see page 92) and Melanzane (see page 118).

1½ aubergines, cut into chunks
20ml garlic oil
salt and freshly ground black pepper

1. Preheat the oven to 200°C/Fan 180°C/Gas 6.

2. Put the aubergines in a roasting tin, drizzle with the oil and toss until everything is nicely coated. Season with salt and freshly ground black pepper.

3. Roast for 20–25 minutes, turning the vegetables halfway through the cooking time. Check that the aubergine is tender – if not, cook for a few more minutes. Leave to cool before using on your pizza.

Roasted Butternut Squash Purée

On our Vegan Zucca (see page 101) we use a base of beautiful, golden butternut squash purée. It's simple to make and tastes gorgeous.

MAKES ABOUT 350G
1 small butternut squash (about 700g),
    cut into quarters lengthways and deseeded
    (no need to peel)
20ml garlic oil
1 rosemary sprig
salt and freshly ground black pepper

1. Preheat the oven to 200°C/Fan 180°C/Gas 6.

2. Place the pieces of squash on a baking tray, flesh-side up, and drizzle with the garlic oil. Add the rosemary and season with salt and pepper.

3. Roast for 30–40 minutes until tender and slightly brown, then remove and set aside until cool enough to handle.

4. Scoop the flesh into a food processor and pulse to break it up. Add a little water, while continuing to pulse, until you have a smooth purée. Taste and add more seasoning if needed.

Roasted Sweet Potato Purée

Sometimes we like a change from passata, so we make this tasty sweet potato purée to use as a base on pizzas such as the Cipollini (see page 120) and Vesuvio (see page 140). It looks beautiful and tastes fantastic.

MAKES ABOUT 350G
2 medium sweet potatoes (about 500g), halved
20ml garlic oil
salt and freshly ground black pepper

1. Preheat the oven to 200°C/Fan 180°C/Gas 6.

2. Place the sweet potato halves on a baking tray, flesh-side up, then drizzle with oil and season with salt and pepper.

3. Roast for 25–30 minutes until tender and slightly brown, then remove and set aside until cool enough to handle.

4. Scoop the flesh into a food processor and pulse to break it up. Add a little water, while continuing to pulse, until you have a smooth purée. Taste and add more seasoning if needed.

Pulled Porchetta

Traditionally, porchetta is a stuffed and rolled pork joint that graces many Italian tables during celebrations. Our version is cooked without stuffing, as it will be shredded when cooked, but it has all the same flavours and textures. We use shoulder, which is a hard-working muscle so really benefits from a long, slow cook, leaving you with meat that is falling apart and meltingly delicious.

MAKES ABOUT 500G
750g boned pork shoulder, skin removed

Marinade
25g olive oil
2 large garlic cloves, peeled and crushed
1 tsp fennel seeds
1 tsp dried or chopped fresh rosemary
1 tsp dried sage
1 tsp lemon zest
1 tsp salt

1. Preheat the oven to 140°C/Fan 120°C/Gas 1.

2. For the marinade, mix the olive oil with the garlic, fennel seeds, herbs, lemon zest and salt in a bowl.

3. Place the pork in a casserole dish, add the marinade and rub it all over the meat. Cover with foil and cook in the oven for 5 hours. At the end of this time, the meat should be so soft you can pull it apart with a spoon.

4. Allow the meat to cool in the dish so it absorbs all the marinade juices before using on your pizza.

Barbacoa Beef

Something magical happens when you slow cook beef shin and brisket – all the chewy bits dissolve away to leave beautifully tender meat that just falls apart. Beef loves a big hit of flavour, so you can pretty much throw anything at it, and when the herbs and spices mix with the meat juices the result is really something special. This is at its best the day after making, so all the flavours can develop and get to know each other.

MAKES ABOUT 1KG
550g boneless beef shin (in one piece)
300g beef brisket (in one piece)

Marinade
400g tin chopped tomatoes
2 medium onions (about 250g),
    peeled and roughly chopped
45g chipotle salsa from a jar
25g fresh coriander, roughly chopped
1 tbsp red wine vinegar
2 tsp soft dark brown sugar
1½ tsp lime juice
1 tsp salt
1 tsp tomato purée
1½ tbsp smoked paprika
2 tsp ground cumin

1. Preheat the oven to 150°C/Fan 130°C/Gas 2. Place the beef in a casserole dish.

2. Put half the tomatoes in a food processor with the onion and all the rest of the marinade ingredients. Blend until smooth, then stir through the rest of the tomatoes.

3. Pour the marinade over the beef, cover the dish with foil and cook for 5½ hours until the meat is so soft you can break it up with a spoon.

4. Allow the meat to cool in the dish so it absorbs all the marinade juices before using on your pizza.

Sloppy Mix

This is the ideal recipe for using up that green pepper in your supermarket mixed pepper pack. It's a key player here in getting the right balance of flavours in the dish. The flavour of a green pepper is a little grassy and slightly bitter compared to a sweet, fruity red pepper, and it is this element that works so brilliantly in the mix. Be warned: cayenne pepper can be deceptively hot, so add with care. You want just enough to add a lovely warmth.

MAKES ENOUGH FOR 2 PIZZAS
3 tbsp olive oil
2 garlic cloves, peeled and very finely chopped
200g minced beef
1 green pepper, deseeded and diced
1 red onion, peeled and finely diced
4 tbsp passata
1 tsp Italian mixed herbs
½ tsp salt
½ tsp paprika
½ tsp cayenne pepper
½ tsp ground cumin

1. Heat the olive oil in a large frying pan over a medium-high heat. Add the garlic and fry for a minute or so until golden, but don't let it burn. Add the mince and cook for 5 minutes until browned, breaking it up with a wooden spoon as it cooks.

2. Add the green pepper and onion and stir for a few minutes over the heat, then add the passata, herbs, salt and spices and mix well. Cook for another 2–3 minutes, then remove the pan from the heat and set aside.

Maple-Glazed Ham Hock

Ham hock comes into its own with a slow cook and a good marinade. It's economical, has plenty of meat on it, and a deep porky flavour that works so well with the sweetness of the maple syrup. If you don't see hocks on display, ask your butcher or order it in advance. When cooking the ham hock, baste it every hour or so, so that a dark, sticky glaze builds up on the meat. Any leftover meat is delicious in a simple salad with a few lentils and a mustardy dressing, or add it to your spaghetti alla carbonara for a fresh twist.

MAKES ABOUT 900G
1.25kg boneless ham hock, skinned

Marinade
125g maple syrup
½ onion, peeled and sliced
2 tbsp lemon juice
3 tsp dark soy sauce
1 tbsp ground ginger
1 tbsp garlic pepper
½ tsp ground cloves
½ tsp ground star anise
freshly ground black pepper, to taste
30ml vegetable oil

1. Preheat the oven to 140°C/Fan 120°C/Gas 1. Place the ham hock in a casserole dish.

2. Put all the marinade ingredients in a food processor and blend until smooth.

3. Pour the marinade over the ham hock. Cover with foil and cook in the preheated oven for 4 hours, basting it every hour or so.

4. Remove the foil, increase the oven temperature to 170°C/Fan 150°C/Gas 3½ then cook for another hour until the ham is so soft you can break it apart with a spoon.

5. Allow the meat to cool in the dish so it absorbs all the marinade juices before using on your pizza.

Pulled Spiced Lamb

When cooked and pulled, this becomes a meltingly tender tangle of soft, juicy lamb and peppers. There's some mild spicing, but if you're not a fan, leave out the red chillies and chilli flakes. Any leftovers can be frozen for another pizza, or try cooking up some pappardelle pasta and mix some of the lamb and peppers through it for a quick dinner.

MAKES ABOUT 600G
750g boneless lamb shoulder (in one piece)

Vegetable mix
1 red pepper, deseeded and sliced
1 green pepper, deseeded and sliced
80g onion, peeled and sliced
3 tbsp lemon juice
20g parsley, roughly chopped
15g red chillies, sliced
1½ tsp salt
2 tsp roughly chopped fresh rosemary
2 tsp chilli flakes

1. Preheat the oven to 140°C/Fan 120°C/Gas 1. Put the lamb in a casserole dish.

2. Put all the vegetable mix ingredients in a bowl and stir until well combined. Tip them over the lamb, cover the casserole dish with foil and cook in the preheated oven for 5 hours, until the meat is soft enough to break up with a spoon.

3. Allow the lamb to cool in the dish so it absorbs all the marinade juices before using on your pizza.

INDEX

PizzaExpress would like to thank the team who worked on this book: thank you to Jamie Orlando Smith for your beautiful photography, Rob Morris who made us more stylish and Alex and Emma of Smith & Gilmour for the elegant design. Also, thank you to Victoria Johnston, Jinny Johnson, Antenor Siqueria, Marlon Prado and Jane Treasure for collating the recipes and writing and testing them for the home cook, and to our agent, Piers Blofeld. We would also like to thank the Orion team, Anna Valentine, Vicky Eribo, Helen Ewing and Shyam Kumar, for making the book happen.

We would like to dedicate this book to all our Pizzaiolos, past and present, who have lovingly handcrafted our pizzas over the years.

First published in Great Britain in 2021 by Seven Dials
an imprint of The Orion Publishing Group Ltd
Carmelite House, 50 Victoria Embankment
London EC4Y 0DZ

An Hachette UK Company

5 7 9 10 8 6 4

Publisher: Vicky Eribo
Project Editor: Jinny Johnson
Editors: Vicky Eribo & Shyam Kumar
Creative Director: Helen Ewing
Design & Art Direction: Smith & Gilmour
Photography: Jamie Orlando Smith
Food & Prop Styling: Rob Morris
Production: Nicole Abel

A CIP catalogue record for this book
is available from the British Library.
ISBN (Hardback) 978 1 8418 8521 6
ISBN (eBook) 978 1 8418 8520 9
Printed and bound in Italy by L.E.G.O. S.p.A.

www.orionbooks.co.uk